NEW VANGUARD 196

WARSHIPS OF THE ANCIENT WORLD

3000–500 BC

ADRIAN K. WOOD ILLUSTRATED BY GIUSEPPE RAVA

First published in Great Britain in 2012 by Osprey Publishing,
Midland House, West Way, Botley, Oxford, OX2 0PH, UK
43-01 21st Street, Suite 220B, Long Island City, NY 11101, USA
E-mail: info@ospreypublishing.com
Osprey Publishing is part of the Osprey Group

© 2012 Osprey Publishing Ltd.

All rights reserved. Apart from any fair dealing for the purpose of private study, research, criticism or review, as permitted under the Copyright, Designs and Patents Act, 1988, no part of this publication may be reproduced, stored in a retrieval system, or transmitted in any form or by any means, electronic, electrical, chemical, mechanical, optical, photocopying, recording or otherwise, without the prior written permission of the copyright owner. Enquiries should be addressed to the Publishers.

A CIP catalogue record for this book is available from the British Library

Print ISBN: 978 1 84908 978 4
PDF e-book ISBN: 978 1 84908 980 7
EPUB e-book ISBN: 978 1 84908 979 1

Index by Mark Swift
Typeset in Sabon and Myriad Pro
Originated by PDQ Digital Media, Bungay, UK

Printed in China through Worldprint Ltd.

13 14 15 16 17   10 9 8 7 6 5 4 3 2 1

www.ospreypublishing.com

Osprey Publishing is supporting the Woodland Trust, the UK's leading woodland conservation charity, by funding the dedication of trees.

DEDICATION

For my mother and the memory of my father, for encouraging a child's interest in history.

GLOSSARY

Aphract – an un-decked ship, usually a galley
Backstay – rope supporting the mast from the rear
Beam – breadth at the widest point of the ship
Bilges – inside of the bottom of the hull of a ship
Boom – spar along the foot of a sail
Bowsprit – spar projecting from the front of a ship
Brails, Brailing ropes – ropes for controlling the amount of sail exposed to the wind
Cataphract – a ship with a fighting deck, usually a galley
Cutwater – a projection from the bow of a ship at the waterline; also 'forefoot'
Diekplous – a tactic of passing through a line of enemy ships followed by a turn and attack from the rear.
Dikrotos – a ship with two banks of oars
Draft – height between the bottom of a ship's keel and the waterline
Forefoot – a projection from the bow of a ship at the waterline; also 'cutwater'
Forestay – rope supporting the mast from the front
Freeboard – height of a ship's side above the waterline
Galley – a ship predominantly powered by oars
Gunwale – uppermost row of planks (or 'strakes') along a ship's side
Halyard – rope for hoisting the sail
Hogging – warping of a ship so that the ends sag down and away from the middle
Hypozomata – ropes attached around the hull to increase structural strength
Interscalmium – the length of a ship's side required for one rower to work his oar
Lift – rope connecting the head of a mast and a yard
Loose-footed – a sail without a boom at the bottom
Monokrotos – a ship with one bank of oars
Mortise and tenon – a method of hull construction involving interlocking pegs and holes
Parablema – screen attached to the side of the ship to prevent the entry of spray and help protect from missiles
Parexeiresia – outrigger for supporting oars
Polis (pl. *poleis*) – (Greek) city-state
Quarter – side of the ship near the stern
Sheet – rope attached to the lower corners of a sail
Shroud – rope supporting the mast from the side
Strakes – planks running horizontally along a ship's side
Thole-pin – vertical peg against which an oar is worked
Yard – horizontal spar(s) from which a sail hangs

CONTENTS

INTRODUCTION   4
- Chronology BCE

EGYPT   5
- Egyptian ships and seafaring
- Warships of Rameses III
- Tactics, organization and the battle of the Delta
- Ships of the Sea Peoples

MINOAN CRETE   15
- The Minoan Thalassocracy
- Minoan ships
- Minoan tactics

BRONZE AGE SYRIA   20
- Ugarit and the Hittites
- Syrian ships
- Tactics and the battle of Alasiya

PHOENICIA: THE LEGACY OF UGARIT   24
- Phoenician sea power
- Phoenician warships
- Phoenician naval practices and tactics

GREECE   30
- Homeric warlords, warriors and ships
- Early pentekonters
- Hekatonters
- Eikosoroi
- Homeric tactics
- Colonial wars (c. 700–500 BCE)
- Late pentekonters
- Triakonters
- Archaic tactics and the battle of Alalia
- Tyrants and sea power
- Polycrates and the Samaina
- The end of an era

BIBLIOGRAPHY   47
- Primary Sources
- Select Secondary Sources Index

INDEX   48

WARSHIPS OF THE ANCIENT WORLD
3000–500 BC

INTRODUCTION

The warships which fought for mastery of the Mediterranean during the Classical period were the culmination of centuries of development. This book traces the naval innovations that culminated in the standardized warships of Greek, Carthaginian and Roman fleets.

The size and general configuration of pre-Classical warships remained comparable throughout the two millennia culminating around 500 BCE. They were required to function as warships as well as conducting trading, piracy and colonization in a period when dedicated warships were rare.

However, two intertwined problems challenge a study of naval warfare in this era: the paucity and disparate nature of the sources and the problems of analysing information thousands of years old. The reconstructions of form and usage that follow are only one possible interpretation of the information. Those interested in alternatives are directed to the bibliography.

Sailing ship on the Nile. The only major difference between Pharaonic and modern times is that the Egyptian square sail has been replaced by the Arab-style triangular sail. The papyrus used in early Egyptian boat construction also provided rope, sailcloth, caulking and matting for side screens which remain largely unchanged to this day. (Photo courtesy of Hazel Wood)

Chronology BCE
c. 3500–3300 Egyptian Predynastic (Gerzean) fresco, possibly world's first naval 'battle' scene
c. 3500–3050 Naval battle depicted on Gebel el-Arak knife takes place
c. 2345–2181 Naval and land forces combine for battle of 'Antelope's Nose'
c. 1991–1782 Egyptian XII Dynasty letter recounting nautical timber is written
19th century Minoans trade across Eastern Mediterranean
1498–1483 Hatshepsut's fleet trades with Punt
1483–1450 Tuthmosis III campaigns in the Levant, securing timber supplies
c. 1470 Centralization of Minoan power at Knossos
14th century Ugarit becomes vassal of, and provides ships for, the Hittites. Tomb of Khenamun, with its paintings of Syrian ships, is built
c. 1316 Uluburun ship wrecked
13th century Gelidonya ship wrecked. Decline of Minoan Crete
1237–1209 Reign of Hittite Tudhaliya IV; conquest of Alasiya
1207 Start of reign of Suppiluliuma II, who led naval attack on Alasiya
12th century Sea Peoples appear in Eastern Mediterranean
1178 or 1175 Battle of the Delta between Egypt and the Sea Peoples
966–926 Solomon involved in maritime trade with Phoenicia, has fleet built
9th century Start of Phoenician hegemony
c. 858–854 Phoenicians under Shalmaneser III battle Tyrian fleet during Tyrian rebellion against Assyrian rule
c. 705 Lelantine War in Greece between Chalcis and Eretria
c. 700 Assyrian attack on Tyre
657–580 Cypselid tyranny in Corinth
c. 600 Phokaia founds colony at Massalia
c. 565 Founding of Phokaian colony of Alalia in Corsica
c. 540–535 Battle of Alalia
538–522 Polycrates' tyranny in Samos
500–494 Ionian revolt against Persia

EGYPT

Egyptian ships and seafaring

The history of Pharaonic Egypt was inextricably linked with the use of boats and ships. From prehistoric times the Nile provided not only food, water and fertility but also a highway, allowing the Egyptians to develop the skills required to construct and utilize water-borne craft. The northerly winds blew opposite to the flow of the Nile, enabling navigation in both directions without the need for rowing. Sail-powered vessels travelling upriver could travel 80 kilometres in a day through a country beset by the hostile tribes living in neighbouring lands.

Though it is not known when they first ventured onto the sea, throughout their history the Egyptians relied on trade with other cultures via the Red and Mediterranean Seas. By the time the Sea Peoples ravaged the Eastern Mediterranean at the end of the Bronze Age, Egypt was able to protect itself by the skilled use of warships, so that the first dateable naval battle and the earliest account of naval tactics come from Egypt.

The Eastern Mediterranean during the late Bronze Age. The migrations of the Dorians moving into Greece and the movement of the Sea Peoples leading up to the battle of the Delta at the start of the 12th century BCE are shown by the arrows. (Map by David Taylor)

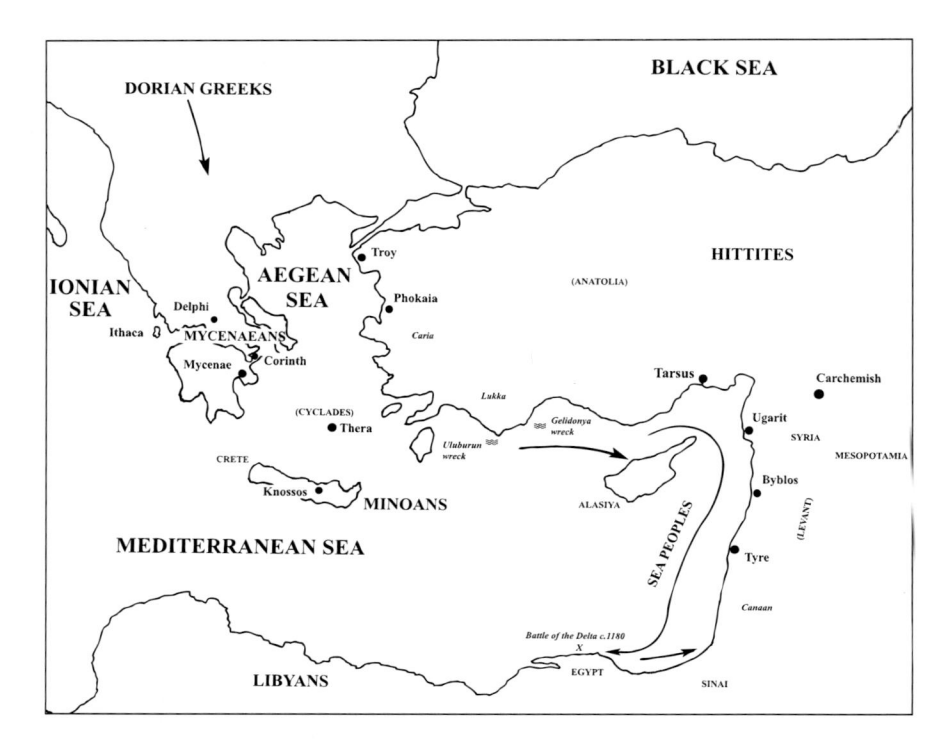

The greatest challenge for Egypt in becoming a naval power was the absence of a supply of suitable timber. This was instrumental in the Egyptians projecting their power onto the sea, since the finest sources of naval timber in the ancient world were found along the coast in the Levant and nearby Cyprus. Timber – mostly cypress and cedar – was imported in the Early Dynastic period and by the middle of the third millennium BCE Egypt traded with Byblos and into Sinai and Punt. It was the necessity of safeguarding annual shipments of wood that led Tuthmosis III to campaign in Phoenicia in the 15th century BCE.

In addition to safeguarding supplies of strategic resources, naval power was essential for suppressing piracy on the Nile since most of Egypt's internal trade and communication was carried out by river. The Nile could serve as a highway for enemies too, unless it was constantly guarded by naval forces. The development of a marine arm to Egypt's military allowed them not only to move troops rapidly along the length of the Nile but also to make amphibious landings, such as that recorded from the Sixth Dynasty when the forces of Pepi I trapped rebellious tribes between land and naval forces at a place called 'Antelope's Nose'.

The first known Egyptian port on the Mediterranean dates from the New Kingdom, but access for shipping through the Delta would have made this unnecessary. Shipyards were established in the Old Kingdom, where specialized carpenters could build a barge in 17 days. In the New Kingdom royal dockyards were established at Per-Nefer, the port of Memphis, which probably served as a base for patrols along both the Nile and the Mediterranean coast.

Though the earliest account of an Egyptian sea battle dates from around 1190 BCE, there are suggestions that it was not the first. A Predynastic tomb fresco from Hierakonpolis shows what may be the world's oldest naval battle scene. Six boats, of two different types, are illustrated alongside men who

Boats on the Nile from Tomb 100 at Hierakonpolis. The painting may depict an early Egyptian military expedition. (From J. E. Quibell and F. W. Green, *Hierakonpolis Part II*, Egyptian Research Account, Fifth Memoir [London 1902], plate LXXV)

appear to be engaged in combat. The fresco has been variously interpreted as a hunt or a ceremonial procession, but it is equally likely that it shows a raid being opposed by Egyptian forces.

An ivory knife handle of uncertain date, though probably Predynastic, illustrates an even more intriguing scene. Two types of boat, one sickle shaped – as early Egyptian vessels often were – the other with symmetrical high prows and sterns believed to be Sumerian, are depicted locked in battle and surrounded by men in combat. Since Egypt and Sumer both conducted maritime trade and the former had a presence on the Red Sea very early in its history, it may indicate that the oldest Near Eastern civilizations conducted naval campaigns against each other, the details of which are now lost.

Warships of Rameses III

Despite a long history of Egyptian warships, the first clear depiction dates from a New Kingdom relief of Rameses III at Medinet Habu. They possess a different configuration to other depictions of Egyptian vessels. The traditional 'spoon-shaped' hull of river craft is gone, though their overall form is still curved. In fact the changes to their hull, rigging and sails represent an intermediate stage between the Egyptian tradition of shipbuilding and that of more 'mainstream' Mediterranean craft. They were influenced by ships of the Levant, the Aegean or Crete, and some later Egyptian nautical terms originated abroad.

Due to their simple construction and a scarcity of quality shipbuilding timber, most early Egyptian vessels were reinforced by rope girdles wrapped around the hull for reinforcement, in addition to great cables running along the inside of the ship from stem to stern to prevent 'hogging' (the ends of the ship sagging away from each other). These were absent on Rameses III's warships, which were built with a stronger internal structure. Small rectangles

The Gebel el-Arak knife, made of flint and hippopotamus ivory. The hilt bears a carving of a naval battle, probably between Sumerians and Egyptians. Though the date the knife was made is not known, it is believed to be as old as the fourth millennium BCE. (Bridgeman)

running below the gunwale may have represented the ends of crossbeams connecting and reinforcing the sides of the ship. Crossbeams could also have been used to support rowing benches, but would have proved an obstacle to the movement of troops in battle unless a gangway was also mounted upon them.

Herodotus [II.96] compared Egyptian boat builders to masons laying bricks, as even in his time most small craft were made of local acacia, which aside from being brittle also provided only small (around 1m) lengths of timber. But since a steady supply of wood from the Levant was a lynchpin of Egyptian strategy, it is likely that at the height of the New Kingdom, Pharaohs had access to enough larger timbers for use in naval shipbuilding.

Excavated Egyptian vessels were made of cedar planks, connected by unlocked mortise and tenon joints, a method of construction that required the hull to be thicker. After the shell was constructed, ribs would be fixed inside and the seams caulked with papyrus or other plant materials. This method allowed a ship to be dismantled, a procedure used to transport vessels across the desert to the Red Sea; at Wadi Gawasis caves were used to store parts of ships. In the Twelfth Dynasty conifer wood (probably pine) was used for masts, juniper for steering oars and ebony for parts in which resistance to wear was important.

The single masts of the warships in the Medinet Habu relief were surmounted by a military-top or crow's nest, rare in the ancient world when masts were struck or disembarked before battle. A single large steering oar replaced the earlier double oar due to the availability of suitable strong timber. The oars, which began to replace paddles in Egyptian vessels in the third millennium, would be passed through rope loops that were mounted on the gunwale below the protective side screens.

Small 'castles' or decks surrounded by bulwarks were positioned at both bow and stern. These provided increased elevation and protection for marines and, in the case of the stern, also served as a seat for the steersman. Rowers were shielded from enemy missiles by a screen that ran along the gunwale, attached at either end to the 'castles'. The stern ornament, shown on earlier ships in the form of a lotus flower, had become a plain sternpost, while the post at the bow was removed and the hull of the ship tapered into a projecting beam carved to resemble the head of a lion. Overall these changes produced a simple and effective warship.

Though on Rameses' relief of the battle of the Delta the sails are furled, it is clear that rigging had developed from traditional Egyptian practices to those used elsewhere in the ancient period. Earlier Egyptian ships had a boom

A — EGYPTIAN WAR GALLEY (TOP) AND SEA PEOPLES SHIP (BOTTOM)

The ships are based on the relief of Rameses III at Medinet Habu. An inscription accompanying the relief speaks of several types of Egyptian vessel assembled at the Delta, but only a single type of warship is depicted. These ships were probably the pride of the Egyptian navy and at the cutting edge of current technology. Though they bear similarities with earlier Egyptian vessels, the rigging, loose-footed sail, transverse beams strengthening the hull and simplified bow and stern decorations make them similar to developments in other Mediterranean cultures. The Sea Peoples' ships possess similarities with the Egyptian galleys (the rigging, side screens, structure of bow and stern platforms), suggesting a common influence on construction. Since the Sea Peoples arrived in Egypt via the Levant these similarities reinforce Egyptian indebtedness to Levantine naval technology.

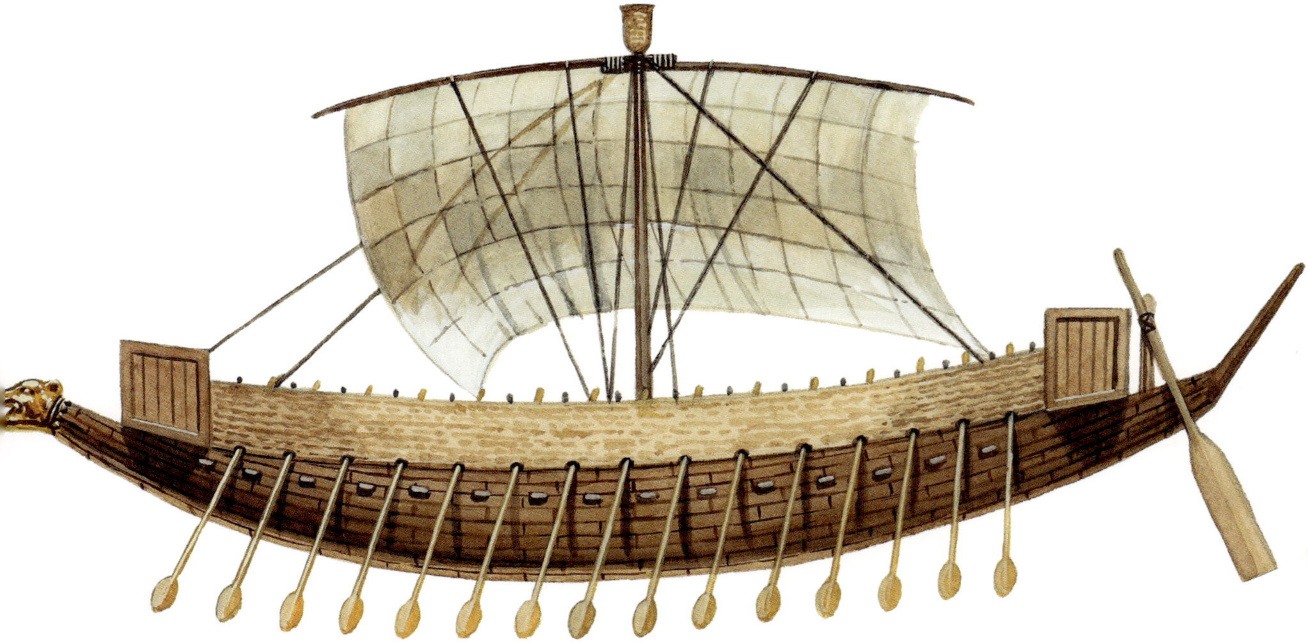

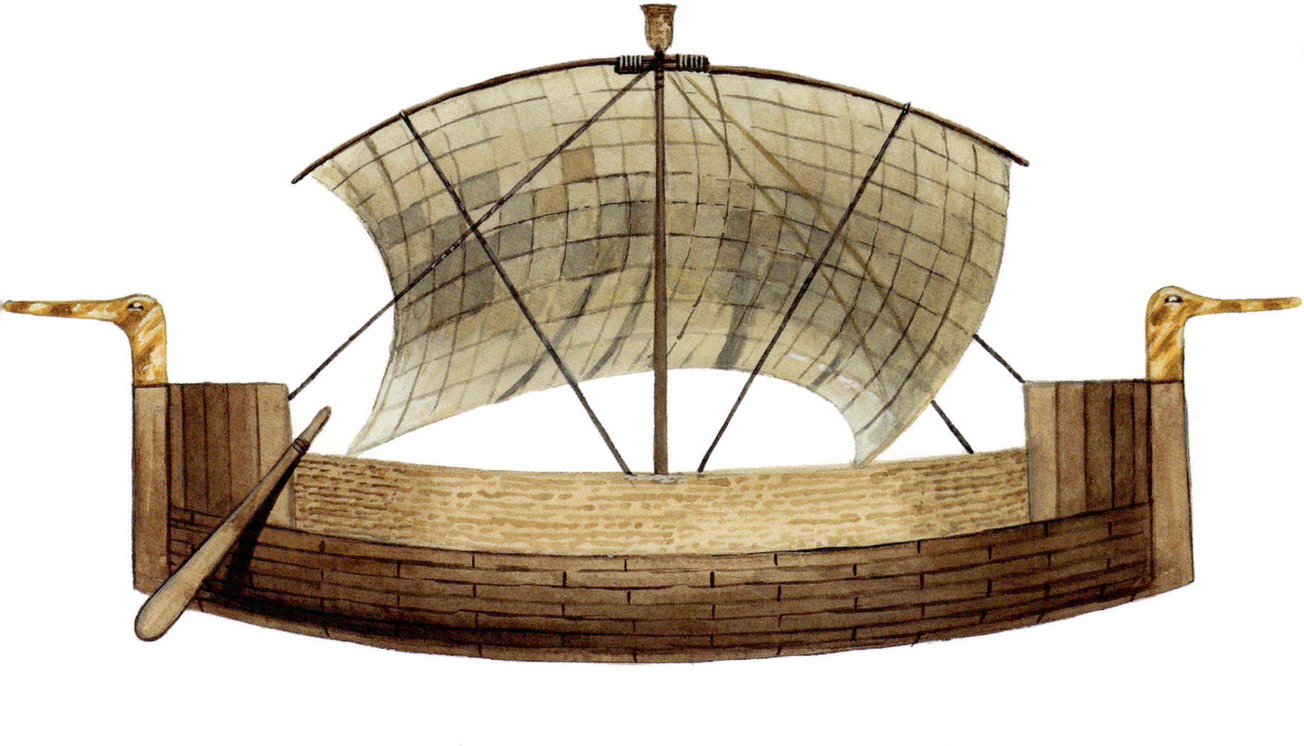

Egyptian boat construction scene c. 2000 BCE from the tomb of Khnumhotep, showing the 'bricklaying' method described by Herodotus. (Drawing by David James Budge after Casson, fig. 11)

at the bottom of the sail, clearly a very ancient practice since the form of two hieroglyphs originated in this feature. But Rameses' warships were 'loose-footed' with the lower corners of the sail controlled by sheets. In addition the radiating brails of earlier ships were replaced by vertical brailing ropes attached at several points along the yard. The yards themselves were constructed of two spars lashed together to save on valuable timber. The mast was supported by a backstay and two forestays, reinforced by halyards between the yard and the gunwales. The cables were woven from halfa grass or papyrus while the sails were still of papyrus or linen since cotton was only just beginning to appear in the Mediterranean at this time.

The four Egyptian vessels on the Medinet Habu relief carry from six to 11 oars on each side, probably due to the artist's lack of space rather than as an accurate numerical representation. Among the rowers are between six and nine marines and a steersman. The marines were depicted larger than the rowers due to the common practice in Egyptian art of representing status by size. Marines armed with bows, spears and maces are positioned in the gangway between the rowers and on the stern castle rather than on a raised deck amidships. Each of the crow's nests is occupied by another marine, who is shown with a mace or sling. It is probable that the fighting crew of Egyptian ships were experienced in naval combat since Rameses III is recorded as manning even cargo ships with archers.

Also aboard the ships are a number of the Sea Peoples, indicated by their two distinctive styles of headgear. They represent captives taken from previously sunken ships, but captives from previous battles probably also served in the Egyptian fleet. After Rameses II defeated the 'Sherden of the Sea' he employed these former enemies as mercenaries. Since they may have been more skilful sailors than Egyptians, they might have been utilized to help sail the ships. In later periods Egypt made considerable use of foreign mercenaries, not only as soldiers but also to man the oars of their ships.

From the reliefs it is apparent that the rowers were specialized and probably highly trained. Other Egyptian illustrations show rowers being whipped, leading to the inevitable question of whether they were slaves, though they may equally be freemen being disciplined in the way sailors were throughout most of history.

Since the number of rowers on Rameses' relief is clearly arbitrary, other Egyptian ships might provide a clue to the true number of oarsmen. The vessels of Queen Hatshepsut a few centuries earlier were depicted much more accurately and to scale and shipped 15 oars to a side. A craft with a crew of 30 rowers (a standard complement for the time) could have carried 15 to 20 marines without becoming unstable and would have reached some 25m in length.

Its form and the poorer quality of its construction would have made such a ship slower than later galleys – perhaps 15–20 per cent slower – but its short length would have provided better acceleration and increased agility, so that it would have turned much more quickly than later vessels. As always, the true measure of a ship's capability would depend on the skill of its crew.

Tactics, organization and the battle of the Delta

The tactics used by Rameses' navy involved archery and the boarding of enemy ships. Grapples are also illustrated in the reliefs and may have been responsible for overturning the capsized enemy vessels by grappling their masts and pulling them over, though the mechanics of this are unclear. It is also uncertain whether the lion-headed prow of the Egyptian craft fulfilled the function of a ram. This feature was positioned higher than the rams of Classical galleys and ramming has been discounted as a possibility. However, 'auxiliary rams' mounted like a prow above the true ram are known from the Classical period and one found at Genoa closely resembles the Egyptian lion's head. It is possible that they were designed to impact the enemy and perhaps stave in their sides, which, in the case of sea-going vessels such as those of the Sea Peoples, probably had a higher freeboard than Egyptian ships. If this was the intention then the ram would have been constructed of, or sheathed in, bronze. In addition, it could have served as a useful boarding platform, particularly if lodged in the hull of an enemy. The division of crew into marines and rowers may support the idea of ramming, as the unarmed rowers would be of no use once the ship was engaged if it was not intended for that purpose. In any event, the absence of a specialized ram would not have prevented ships from driving into the sides of the enemy and perhaps capsizing them. Finally it is worth noting that the battle of the Delta also involved the use of land-based archery to support the ships as a way of bringing more Egyptian firepower to bear on the invaders.

The size of Egypt's fleet in this period is not known, though if the size of its armies – and its navies in later times – is any indication, they would have been substantial; Egypt's wealth was legendary. During peacetime ships could be dismantled or laid up, common practice in ancient times, or used for anti-piracy patrols along the coasts or the Nile. There is reference to a 'Chief of the Royal Ships' who may have served as an admiral, while individual temples bestowed similar titles, such as 'Chief of the Ships of the House of Ptah'. It is likely that just as they dominated other aspects of Egyptian life, the temples also provided ships for Egypt's navy.

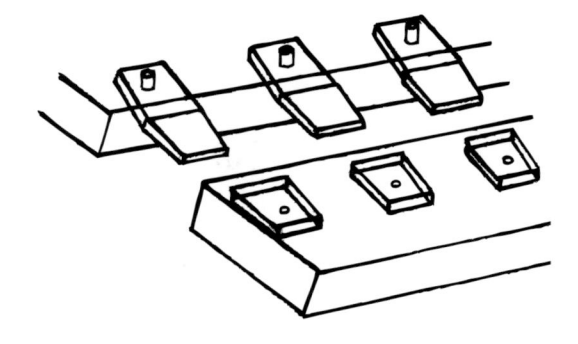

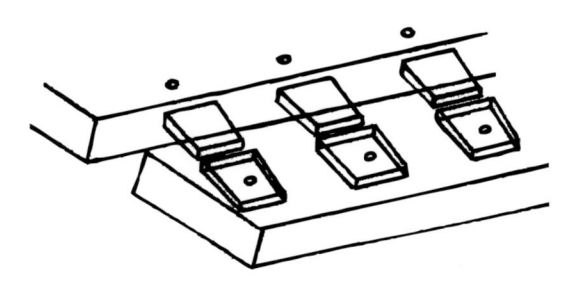

Pegged mortise and tenon joint, the standard method of ship construction in the ancient world. The tenons (projections) fit into the mortises (holes) and are locked in place by pegs, which pass through the walls of the mortise and the body of the tenon. (Drawing by the author after McGrail, fig. 27)

OVERLEAF
A mural from the tomb of Sennefer (1567–1320 BCE) in Thebes showing a boat on the Nile. The vessel bears similarities to the warships on the Medinet Habu carvings, notably the bow and stern platforms, the similarity of the steering oar, the shape of the bow and the use of oars rather than paddles. The rigging is more accurately depicted in this image than in Rameses' carvings and reveals the major difference between the two vessels – the boom at the foot of the sail. (Bridgeman)

Ships of the Sea Peoples

The naval victory commemorated in the Medinet Habu reliefs came at the expense of the Sea Peoples, a confederation of tribes or groups of uncertain origin, though some were Greek or Aegean. At the beginning of the 12th century BCE they were involved in the collapse of the Hittite empire and spread a swathe of destruction across Syria, Palestine and Cyprus. Their appearance was more of a migration than a military campaign and it seems they sought land rather than plunder.

B BATTLE OF THE DELTA

This plate is based on the relief at Medinet Habu, which shows a chaotic battle with the ships of both sides intermingled. The Egyptian vessels manoeuvred under oars, capsizing enemy ships while their superior archery 'cleared the decks', making the work of the Sea Peoples in controlling their ships all but impossible. Though square sails were not ideal for manoeuvring, research has shown that they allowed ships to sail fairly close to the wind. However, sails were a liability in battle, which is why both sides fought with sails reefed. The lack of long-range missile weapons that could compete with Egyptian bows was disastrous for the Sea Peoples. Incapable of exploiting the ferocity in mêlée that had allowed them to overrun other civilizations of the Near East, the invaders lacked any advantage unless it was the greater number of their ships.

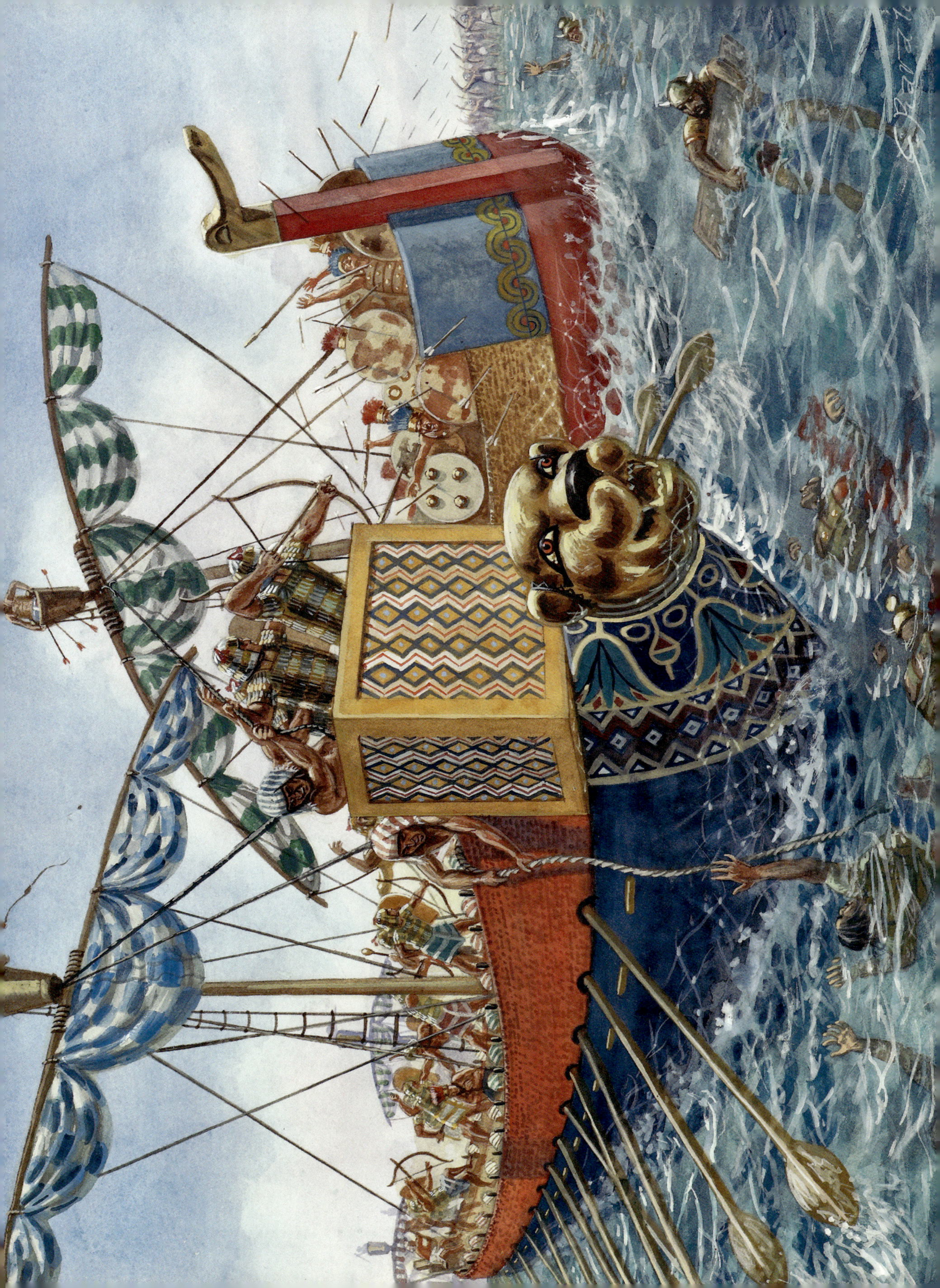

Inscription of Rameses at Medinet Habu:
'I was prepared and armed to [trap] them like wild fowl... I went forth, directing these marvellous things. I equipped my frontier in Zahi, prepared before them. The chiefs, the captains of infantry, the nobles, I caused to equip the river mouths, like a strong wall, with warships, galleys, and barges. They were manned from bow to stern with valiant warriors bearing their arms, soldiers of all the choicest of Egypt, being like lions roaring upon the mountain tops.
As for those who had assembled before them on the sea, the full flame was in their front, before the river mouths, and a wall of metal upon the shore surrounded them. They were dragged, overturned, and laid low upon the beach; slain and made heaps from stern to bow of their galleys, while all their things were cast upon the water. [Thus] I turned back the waters to remember Egypt; when they mention my name in their land, may it consume them...'

The ships shown on the reliefs bore similarities to those of their Egyptian foes but also a number of differences; they were distinctly symmetrical like the Syrian ships of two centuries earlier but their bow- and stern-posts were more angular, terminating in curious duck-headed decorations. Like the Egyptian warships they had castles at bow and stern, a mast with a single yardarm and a crow's nest, and screens along the gunwales. The rig and furled sail were the same as those of the Egyptians, but were depicted without oars.

The Sea Peoples' ships appear to lack oars. Rameses' inscription implies that the enemy were overconfident and scholars have suggested they must have been surprised by the Egyptian forces and unable to run their oars out. This is doubtful, as they were prepared enough to equip themselves with weapons and armour. It is more likely, taking into account that the Egyptians were clearly divided into fighting and rowing crew, that the entire complement of the Sea Peoples' ships was combatant. This was normal throughout history for ships crewed by warriors or pirates. Like the Vikings or Homer's Achaeans they would row until action was imminent, then ship oars and arm themselves to fight.

The Sea Peoples' crews were armoured in the familiar fashion of their kind, with two distinctive types of helmet and many wearing armour of strips of leather or hide covering the torso. They carried spears and triangular straight swords, and many had round shields.

It is apparent that though they might have been fierce warriors, they faced several disadvantages in this battle. The Egyptian ships manoeuvred under oars and could select when and where to fight the Sea Peoples' stationary vessels, or avoid contact at all, allowing their famed archers to shoot from a distance. The Sea Peoples were not shown with missile weapons and very many of them are shown pierced with arrows. They were probably equipped for fighting on land, their ships intended only to carry them to the shore. Faced with the manoeuvrability and archery of the Egyptians it is not surprising that they were defeated.

Too little information has survived to reconstruct a Sea Peoples ship in any detail, if – since they were a force gathered from disparate geographic and cultural areas – their vessels were anything more definite than a vague type. They were probably constructed in the same fashion as Aegean or Syrian rather than Egyptian ships of their era and their form would resemble vessels of a similar shape and function, such as Viking ships, seen throughout history.

Part of the relief erected by Rameses III at Medinet Habu. In this view the mason has attempted to depict the chaos and carnage of the battle. To the left is an Egyptian war galley, with some of the crew dragging prisoners from the water while to the right the surviving crew of a Sea Peoples ship are unable to respond to Egyptian archery. (Alamy)

MINOAN CRETE

The Minoan Thalassocracy

> Minos, according to tradition, was the first person to organize a navy. He controlled the greater part of what is now called the [Aegean] Sea; he ruled over the Cyclades, in most of which he founded the first colonies, putting his sons in as governors after having driven out the Carians. And it is reasonable to suppose that he did his best to put down piracy in order to secure his own revenues.
>
> Thucydides [I.4]

Minoan Crete was first and foremost a mercantile empire which from its rise around the start of the second millennium traded with Egypt, the Levant, the Aegean, and beyond to Italy, Sicily and perhaps as far as Spain and the

The Minoan port of Kato Zakros (or 'Zakro') on the east coast of Crete. This settlement was ideally situated for trade with Anatolia, the Levant, Cyprus and Egypt. Syrian ivory and Cypriot copper have been found here. (Photo courtesy of Dr Wendy Austin-Giddings)

Frescoes showing Cretan ships from Thera dating from the height of Minoan power (*c.* 1650–1500 BCE). The vessels on these frescoes suggest a variety of purposes – trade, celebration and war – but the type and configuration of the vessels are remarkably consistent, showing that this kind of ship formed the backbone of Minoan fleets. (Bridgeman)

Atlantic. Its ships needed to carry cargo and also to defend themselves and support Minoan trading colonies. Aside from the dangers of trading on foreign shores, Crete shared the Eastern Mediterranean with Egypt, the states of the Levant and southern Anatolia and the growing power of Mycenae. Though the Minoan *thalassocracy* has sometimes been portrayed as a period of stability and peace, it is inconceivable that friction between these competing powers did not result in conflict. For such confrontations Crete was well placed strategically and well supplied with good anchorages (such as at Kolymba where a 960m^3 harbour was sawn from native rock) and shipbuilding timbers so that most of its cities were built close to the sea and were largely unfortified. As Ovid [*Metamorphoses* IX:439–516] says, 'When Minos was in his prime, his very name terrified great nations.'

How the Minoan navy was organized and supported is unknown. Initially Crete was composed of city-states but around 1470 BCE power became centralized at Knossos. This change need not have altered the basic structure

The caldera of Santorini, southernmost of the Cyclades islands in the Aegean. Though over 100km from Crete, the town of Thera was culturally Minoan and was destroyed by a volcanic eruption, which was connected with the decline of Minoan civilization. (Photo courtesy of Dr Wendy Austin-Giddings)

of Crete's trading and naval activities. Local lords (*guasileus*, forerunners of Homer's *basileus*) controlled 'leaders of the war hosts' (*lawagetas*) who led retinues of followers or *hequetai*, men wealthy enough to own chariots and serve as elite forces. There are also clear signs that mercenaries were utilized. An image of a Cretan leading what are probably Nubians has been found while Herodotus [I.171] relates that: 'The Carians ... were subjects of Minos ... they never paid tribute in money but manned his ships... Minos had great military success and extended his conquests over a wide area...' The story of Theseus confirms that later Greeks remembered Minoan Crete as a state that took their sons and daughters as slaves.

Minoan seal-stone carved with an image of a ship. The ship has a bifurcated stem on a typical Minoan rising prow, and the common diamond-shaped crosshatching representing the sail. The Minoans used these gems to stamp an image in clay or wax. (Author's collection)

Minoan ships

Many representations of Minoan ships have survived and depict a number of similar forms. They are slender and have rounded hulls that rise in gentle curves and straighten towards the end of both bow and stern. Some vessels are higher at the stern, others at the bow, while others are almost symmetrical. Many prows terminate in a bi-, tri- or quadri-furcation or in an arrowhead. Steerage was controlled by one or sometimes two steering oars. In addition, some ships carried a projection at the stern above the waterline, the forerunner of the later Greek *holkaion* which served as a boarding ramp when the ship was beached and may also have provided leverage to assist launching.

Along with this standard type, a few ships appear asymmetrical with the projecting forefoot of later Greek vessels. Theories that these are a particular type employed for rapid amphibious raids cannot be discounted, but their rarity suggests that they did not form a significant part of Minoan sea power and may represent a localized tradition.

Frescoes from Thera show ships bedecked with decoration for what may be a triumphal entry into port. These include lines between the masthead and either end of the vessel carrying bunting, curious decorations in the form of

A reconstructed Minoan vessel, now in the Maritime Museum in Chania, Crete, showing the sail footed with a boom, a distinctive feature of many Minoan ships. The gangway is mounted upon the rowing benches, providing height during boarding actions. Note that in the absence of dedicated storage, the oars are laid across the gunwale. (Alamy)

The Troodos Mountains of Cyprus. These forested mountains, along with the hills of Phoenicia, provided the ancient world with much of the timber used for ship construction by surrounding civilizations. Cyprus was also probably the location of Alasiya, site of the naval victories of the Hittite king Suppiluliuma II. (Photo courtesy of Hazel Wood)

stars or animals atop the bowsprit (which may have been a form of identification) and canopied areas amidships and at the stern behind the steersman.

A single mast amidships supported a broad, shallow sail woven of linen or Egyptian papyrus. It was supported by a yardarm and boom, each controlled by a pair of lifts. Braces leading to the steersman suggest that he was responsible for controlling the set of the sails and some depictions show stays fore and aft. The mast was lowered onto either a crutch or the stanchions supporting the central canopy.

The largest vessels depicted carry 30 oarsmen. Some of the ships from Thera are shown with many men paddling, though this may be showing slaves made to paddle for the ships' triumphant return to port. Some, apparently cargo vessels, carry neither oars nor paddles, though otherwise they closely resemble the oared ships in hull form and rig.

A replica of a Minoan ship, the *Minos*, has been constructed in Crete using traditional techniques. The hull (17m long and 4m wide internally) was constructed of cypress trunks split in two, which were used for opposite sides of the ship to ensure symmetry. They were glued with resin and secured by nearly 800m of rope. The sides of the ship were held apart by an 'A'-shaped frame laid horizontally in the bow. The hull was covered with linen coated with conifer resin that was then whitened with lime to serve as a base for the colourful painted decorations depicted at Thera. It was intended to carry 30 oarsmen along with a captain, two steersmen and two sailors and may well be typical of the size and type of ship used in war by the Minoans.

Minoan tactics

Some conclusions may be drawn about the tactics of the Minoan navy. Arrowheads have been found at Minoan sites and in the Classical period Crete provided numerous accomplished mercenary bowmen. So though archery is not shown aboard ship it is likely that the tactic was commonplace. One damaged fresco shows ships, one of which is capsized, in what was probably a sea battle. A man at the prow of the ship holds what appears to be a pike. Long spears or pikes are well known from Minoan art and they may also be seen stowed under the canopy of ships at Thera, along with boar's-tusk helmets. Pikes would be ideal for boarding actions and used to fend off enemy ships. The flexible structure of Minoan ships does not suggest that ramming was commonplace and their lengthy prows seem to confirm this, but since enemy ships probably had a similar structure it cannot be discounted. The Minoans were skilled sailors so it is unlikely that enemies would choose to confront them at sea in a battle of manoeuvre. In fact Minoan sea power is one reason why many Aegean towns were fortified and positioned on high ground away from the water's edge. The majority of actions fought probably consisted of amphibious landings and raids in which their long spears, huge shields and high quality swords might give them an advantage.

Detail of a red figure *krater* from Rhodes. Dating from the 13th to 12th century BCE, the painting shows warriors in Mycenaean dress and equipment. During this period the Mycenaean influence spread across the former Minoan empire, and its warriors may even have travelled on Ugaritic ships to fight for the Hittites. (Bridgeman)

BRONZE AGE SYRIA

During the Bronze Age the most important maritime Mediterranean region was Syria. It sat at the crossroads of trade routes from Egypt, Mesopotamia, Cyprus and Anatolia and was occupied by a variety of empires seeking to benefit from its trade and strategic location. Throughout the period it controlled the two most important military commodities, timber and bronze. Shipbuilding timber was obtained from Cyprus and from the hills of the Levant, areas still essential to the successor navies a millennium later. The wrecks of two vessels excavated on the southern coast of Turkey have revealed that tonnes of copper and tin and the tools, materials and expertise to work them were traded across the whole of the Eastern Mediterranean. Personal effects of the crews suggest that the ships originated in Syria, which 14th and 13th century Egyptian artists considered the home of bronze working.

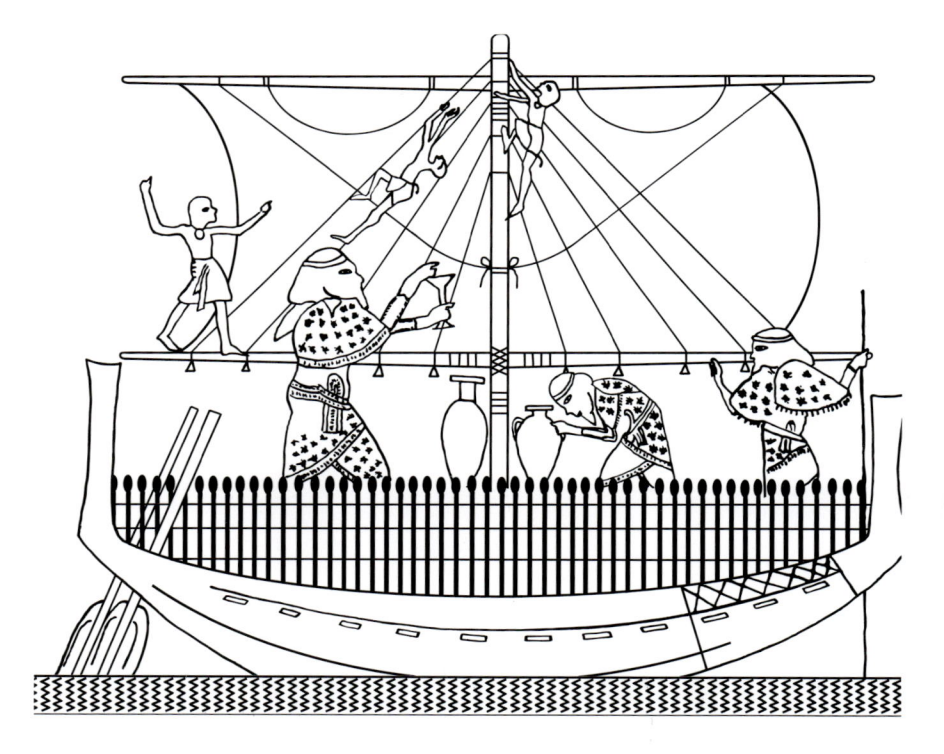

Mycenaean bronze spearheads dating from the end of the second millennium BCE. The Mycenaeans were the foremost arms manufacturers of the late Bronze Age and their weapons have been found across the Eastern Mediterranean. It is likely that along with their weapons the Mycenaeans also provided mercenaries. (Author's collection)

Detail of a 14th century painting from the tomb of Khanamun, showing Syrian ships unloading in an Egyptian port. The rigging and the distinctive rounded and reinforced hull of a robust seagoing vessel are clearly visible. (Drawing by David James Budge after Davis and Faulkner)

C — SYRIAN SHIP (TOP) AND MINOAN GALLEY (BOTTOM)

The Syrian ship is of a type which would have been provided by Ugarit for the use of the city's Hittite overlords and to defend against the attacks of the Sea Peoples. The majority of ships used in war were multi-purpose, in this case a merchantman which could be militarized when the occasion demanded. The sturdy structure and broad beam would allow it to travel across open water and survive rough seas, though the wrecks at Uluburun and Gelidonya show that this was not always the case. The Minoan ship is one example of a broad family of vessels known to have been used in Bronze Age Crete. Though the two are roughly contemporary, it was of a very different type to the Syrian vessel, the Minoan ship originating in slender oar- or paddle-powered craft more suggestive of piracy and amphibious attacks than of trading. Its structure was much lighter and relied for survival on flexibility rather than the strength of construction. Awnings above the rowers or steersman were often used and were part of the decoration beloved of Minoan sailors, in addition to providing protection against the elements.

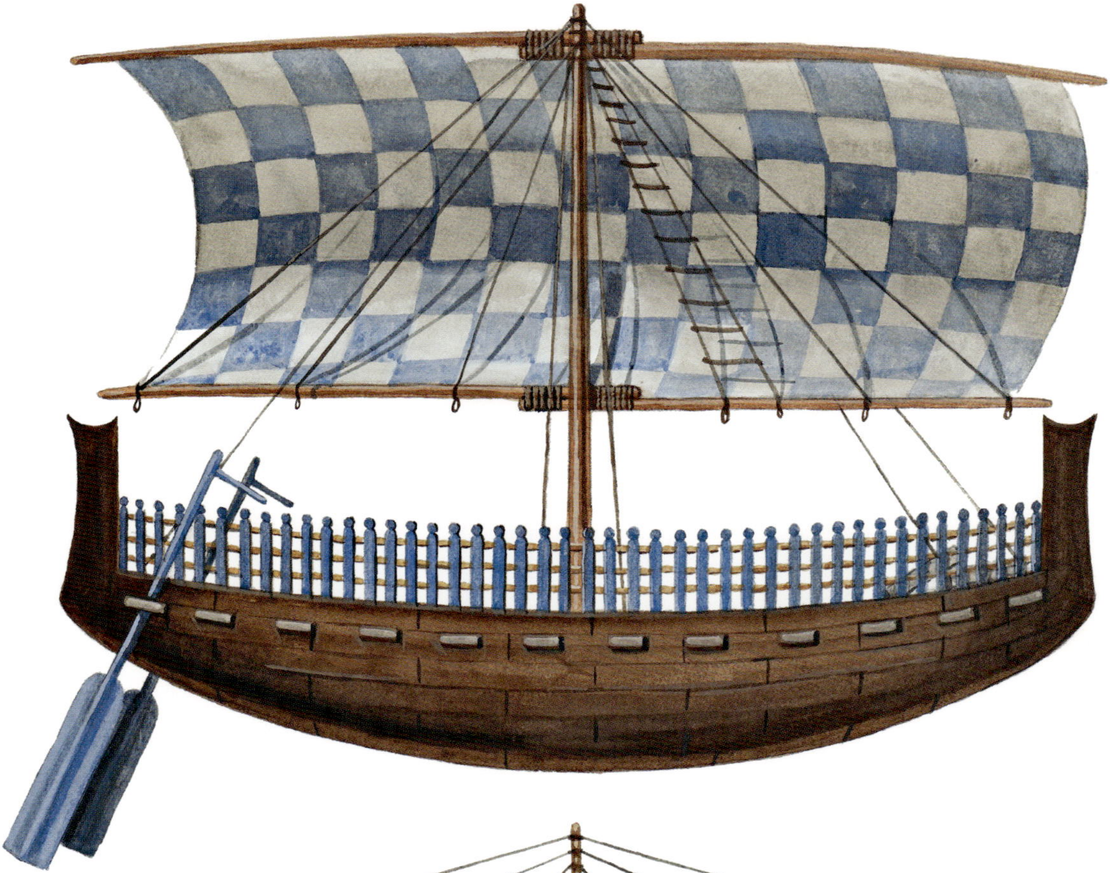

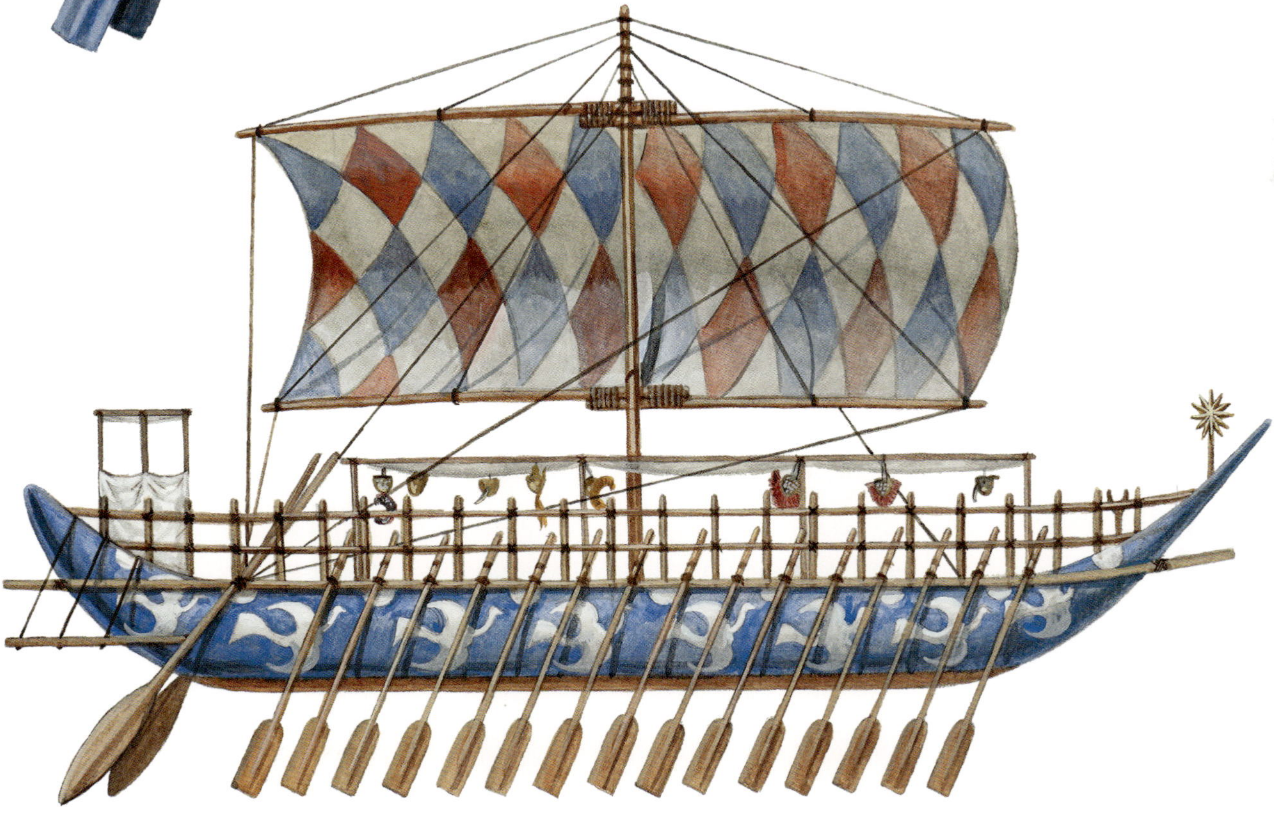

Ingots taken from the Uluburun wreck, now on display in the Underwater Archaeology Museum in Bodrum. Ingots of these types are known to have been traded across the Mediterranean and surrounding lands and, along with timber, were the strategic material that fuelled the wars of the period. (Alamy)

Ugarit and the Hittites

The most important 'city-state' at this time was Ugarit. Ugarit's wealth and strategic location made it indispensable to local land empires, most famously the Hittites. Based in the heart of Anatolia, the Hittites lacked naval forces to deal with enemies on the surrounding coasts. In the 14th century BCE Ugarit, which could man 150 ships, became a vassal providing them with a fleet. When incursions of the Sea Peoples ('the people of Shikala who live in boats') began to be felt on the Syrian coast, the last king was forced to write to an ally that, '... all my troops and chariots are in the Land of Hatti, and all my ships are in the Land of Lukka.' Lukka (Lycia) was a perennial problem for the Hittites, partly due to its connections with Ahhiyawa (the Mycenaean Aegean), and Ugarit seems to have been responsible for keeping the sea in the area secure and for transporting Ahhiyawan mercenaries to join Hittite armies.

Syrian ships

The ships used by the Hittite army and for the protection of Syrian trade were not dedicated warships. A ship of the type used can be reconstructed from both contemporary merchant vessels sunk at Uluburun and Gelidonya and 14th century Egyptian tomb paintings showing Syrian traders.

The hulls shown on the 'Khenamun' paintings were rounded and similar to Egyptian vessels of the time, with two notable differences. The stem and sternposts of the Syrian vessels rose vertically, in a design similar to the ships of the Sea Peoples, and ended in concave indentations. More importantly they were not braced with the rope trusses found on Egyptian vessels, showing that the hulls of Syrian seagoing ships were significantly stronger. The sunken ships revealed that the construction was 'shell-first', with the planks fastened to the keel and to each other with pegged mortise and tenon joints. These fastenings were large, some of the mortises as deep as 17cm with pegs 2cm in diameter, resulting in a robust hull. The keel of the Uluburun wreck was constructed of

The coastline of south-west Anatolia is characterized by rugged hills, inlets and islands. In poor weather the sea becomes treacherous to ships and this was no different in ancient times. Both of the famous Bronze Age wrecks, those of Gelidonya and Uluburun, were found in this area. (Photo courtesy of Robert Grimley)

fir-wood and the tenons of oak. The projecting ends of crossbeams are also visible on the paintings. Rising from the gunwales were rails, perhaps fitted with screens that would help keep cargo and crew dry, and in battle provide protection from missiles. This basic structure was still in use a millennium later.

A single sail was supported by a yard of two lashed spars at the top and a boom at the bottom. On each side of the ship five ropes connected the boom to the junction of the mast and the yard, while rope ladders led up to the masthead. The yard curved gently downward, unlike Egyptian ships, though the rig was otherwise similar. The ship was controlled by a pair of steering oars with large square blades.

The Uluburun wreck included 24 anchor stones, apparently deployed in pairs. The great number of anchors, which relied for their effectiveness on weight alone rather than on the familiar modern 'anchor' shape, shows that securing the ship at sea was a complex and demanding process. The gangplanks shown on the paintings were probably carried on board the ship and may have been used in the case of boarding actions.

The Uluburun vessel, a coastal trader, was some 9m in length, but a contemporary document refers to ships able to carry upward of 225 tonnes of grain. Ships of this design could easily have stretched to 20m or more. Their length-to-beam ratio might approach 5:1 since they sacrificed speed for structural strength, stability and capacity, necessary for the transport of soldiers.

Tactics and the battle of Alasiya

In the years before the destruction of Hatti and Ugarit, a campaign was conducted by the last Hittite king against Alasiya. The text of a clay tablet relates how:

> ... I mobilized and I, Suppiluliuma, the Great King, immediately [crossed?] the sea. The ships of Alasiya met me in the sea three times for battle, and I smote them; and I seized the ships and set fire to them in the sea. But when I arrived on dry land, the enemies from Alasiya came in multitude against me for battle.

A reconstruction of the Uluburun wreck, showing the distinctive stempost, the steering oar and the curving lines that show this vessel as a 'roundship', that is one not primarily intended for war. It was this style of ship that would have carried the Hittites of Suppiluliuma to Alasiya. (Alamy)

A number of strategic and tactical points are apparent. The forces fielded by both sides must have been substantial, requiring three naval battles before the Hittite-manned ships could land. The mention of seizing the enemy vessels suggests that boarding was the tactic used, in which the Hittites with their history of almost constant warfare would excel. Had they been a maritime power it is likely that they would not have burned the enemy ships after capture, but would instead have made use of them for their own fleet. Suppiluliuma's father, Tudhaliya IV, had conquered Alasiya and taken its people as captives, so whether Suppiluliuma fought natives or recently arrived Sea Peoples it made sense to deny them a fleet with which they could cause further problems.

PHOENICIA: THE LEGACY OF UGARIT

The convulsions that brought down the Bronze Age civilizations left a power vacuum in the Eastern Mediterranean. Despite the destruction caused by the Sea Peoples, Levantine cities recovered sufficiently to dominate the seas of the region before the end of the 9th century BCE. Ugarit never recovered but Tyre, Sidon, Byblos, Arvad and others soon became wealthy and powerful for the same reasons that had allowed Ugarit to become so important.

Surprisingly little is known about the Phoenicians; even their name comes from a Greek word, meaning 'red men', a reference to the murex dye for which they were famed. Most of what is known was written by their Greek and Roman enemies, whose authors often belittled Phoenician achievements and character. Nevertheless the Greeks learned a great deal from them, especially in maritime affairs, contributing to the birth of Greece's Classical 'golden age'. In Homer, Phoenicians have a monopoly on trade in the Aegean and are feared and envied for their sea power.

Phoenician sea power

The kingdoms which controlled the Eastern Mediterranean from the 9th century BCE until the time of Alexander in many ways resembled later Greek *poleis*. The city of Tyre can be seen as a blueprint for the colonies the Phoenicians established overseas: a defensible island with protected anchorages and access to mainland agriculture. Perhaps because of this, Phoenicia was rarely unified (though Tyre and Sidon were always the primary states), cities being defined by their independence and sea power. Even when the region fell under the sway of the Assyrians, Tyre was left in a condition of semi-autonomy since it provided both access to trade and a navy. The Phoenicians were both hated and admired by local peoples. They aided Solomon in the conduct of trade and construction of a navy, while the Book of Ezekiel [27] says: 'Who is there like Tyre ... thy wares went forth out of the seas, thou fillest many peoples: thou didst enrich the kings of the earth with thy merchandise and thy riches ... thou art become a terror...'

Elsewhere in the Hebrew Bible the power of the Phoenicians was associated with their ships. They disseminated metal-working and shipbuilding technologies, but their greatest legacy was the breadth of their maritime ventures, which made a single entity of the Mediterranean. They traded with – and founded settlements in – Cyprus, Cilicia, Lycia, Sicily, Sardinia, North Africa and Spain. They also ventured into the Atlantic, trading tin from the British Isles and perhaps amber from the Baltic, and later circumnavigated Africa. But the Phoenicians were not solely merchants. Their trading enclaves grew into powerful colonies which extended their control over nearby

ABOVE, LEFT
The flight of the king of Tyre from the Assyrians, c. 700 BCE. This carving shows two types of Phoenician ship, one with a ram and one without. Both types bear a fighting deck and so both are believed to have been designed to serve as warships. Notable are two banks of oars positioned one above the other (*dikrotos*) and the soldiers positioned along with refugees on the fighting deck. (Bridgeman)

ABOVE, RIGHT
The ruins of Arwad in the north of the ancient region of Phoenicia. Arwad was settled early in the second millennium BCE and continued to flourish to the end of the Phoenician period. It was an important trade centre and was actively involved in the struggles between Egypt, Anatolia and Mesopotamia. Like Tyre it was situated on an easily defensible island close to land. (Photo courtesy of Phoenicia.org)

hinterlands. In a 9th century inscription a Tyrian commander boasts about how his troops devastated Cyprus, and when the Greeks began to send out colonies beyond the Aegean, friction arose that did not cease until after the fall of the greatest Tyrian colony, Carthage. So determined were these armed traders to maintain the monopoly on their trade that Strabo [iii.5.11] reported a Phoenician captain running his ship aground and drawing his enemies after him rather than allow them to gain knowledge of their routes.

Phoenician warships

Illustrations of Phoenician warships have survived, in particular a relief from the palace of Sennacherib at Khorsabad. This shows warships and sailing ships with two banks of oars, both in some detail, fleeing an attack on Tyre in around 700 BCE. In addition several wrecks of Phoenician ships have been excavated and a replica of a merchantman, the *Phoenicia*, has been constructed using local materials and traditional techniques. Along with documentary evidence these allow a reconstruction of Phoenician warships of this time.

The hull was constructed using mortise and tenon joints (called *coagmenta punicana* by the Romans) fastened in place by iron nails or wooden pegs. While iron rapidly oxidizes in sea water, the Phoenicians pioneered the use of bitumen to coat their hulls, protecting the iron and waterproofing the vessel. Ezekiel relates that the planks were of fir. In the later Marsala wrecks writing was found on many of the individual hull components suggesting that warships were assembled from a 'kit' of parts. The technique may well date back to the height of Phoenician power. A cutwater, which may have doubled as a ram, is visible on the relief, apparently separate from the hull. This is confirmed by the construction of the Marsala ships where the ram is attached only by iron nails and so could easily have been removed. A separate ram eased construction, allowed dismantling of the ship for repairs or for transport across land, and ensured that the shock of impact in battle was absorbed by the ram instead of transferring all of the force to the hull.

Both types of ships on the Khorsabad relief carried two banks of oars, though another carving shows a similar galley with just one bank. The upper oars were rowed over the gunwale and the lower through oar ports, the banks offset to reduce the height of the hull. Between the two a line is visible which may represent either a widening of the hull or an outrigger.

Part of an Assyrian frieze depicting a Phoenician warship under oars. Among the innovations visible on the relief are the two banks of oars and the high fighting-deck protected by a bulwark and hung with shields. Also noticeable is the band around the base of the ram, illustrating that it was either separate from the keel or sheathed in bronze. (Author's collection)

The replica ship *Phoenicia* under sail. The sail is dyed in 'Tyrian purple', the dye extracted from the murex for which Phoenicia was famous throughout the ancient world. The lifts used to raise and lower the sail and the forestay (connecting the mast-top to the prow) and part of the backstay are visible. (Photo courtesy of Phoenicia.org)

The number of oars shown varied from eight to 11, but most likely represented a larger number. Phoenician oars were constructed of oak.

A cedar mast supported a sail (shown reefed to the yard) and was itself supported by a backstay and two forestays. Four other cables are shown, probably sheets or braces. Phoenician sails were of Egyptian linen and ropes were woven of white flax.

The most curious feature of the Khorsabad warships was the high fighting-deck. The ships in the relief are stylized and shortened due to artistic convention, but a high deck required a stable ship to prevent capsizing. The fighting-deck was mounted on stanchions inside the line of the rowers, and ran along the length of the vessel but not across its full beam. The ship would need a greater beam-to-length ratio for stability and to carry more supplies, particularly since Phoenician warships would undertake longer journeys than the short coast-hugging trips of Classical triremes. A reconstruction requires a length of at least 18m and a beam of perhaps 3m, resulting in a ratio of 6:1. Under oars this ship would make less speed than a comparable later ship of the same number of oars, but was compensated by greater height for archery and boarding actions.

The replica Phoenician ship *Phoenicia* during construction. At this stage the hull has already been constructed with planks laid edge-to-edge. The bow- and stern-posts and the first transverse strengthening ribs inside the hull are in position. (Photo courtesy of Phoenicia.org)

Phoenician naval practices and tactics

No account survives of Phoenician naval tactics before the Persian conquest, but their vessels were equipped with a cutwater which could have been used for ramming, if that was not in fact its primary purpose. The most important factors in ramming were the skill of the crew and the quality of ship construction. Phoenicians were renowned as the ancient world's greatest sailors. The Sidonians were the best sailors in Xerxes' fleet and he travelled in a Sidonian ship, while Sennacherib of Assyria ordered the construction of 'Mighty ships [after] the workmanship of their hand, they built dextrously, Tyrian, Sidonian and Cypriot sailors, captives of my hand, I ordered [to descend] the Tigris with them...' As for their ships themselves, Xenophon [*Oeconomicus* VIII.14] quotes Ischomachus as saying, 'I think that the best and most perfect arrangement of things I ever saw was when I went to look at the great Phoenician sailing vessel.'

In later times Sidonian ships performed peacetime patrols to keep the Eastern Mediterranean clear of pirates, an activity with no doubt a long history. Phoenicians pioneered the use of the Pole Star (*Phoinike* in Greek), which enabled them to navigate at night, a capability of obvious strategic value.

As for the use of tactics beyond the manoeuvring of ships for ramming, it is likely that the Phoenicians used foreigners for boarding actions; the small population of colonies made the use of mercenaries essential. Aside from the

D **EVACUATION FROM TYRE**

When Sargon II of Assyria assaulted Tyre with an army claimed to number 200,000, the Tyrian king fled by sea, though the city did not immediately fall. Two types of ship are shown on the Assyrian relief of this event, one with the ram-like cutwater and one without, leading to the conclusion that a ram was used on vessels operating predominantly as warships. Both types possess the elevated 'fighting deck' to provide marines with a height advantage in battle. It is noteworthy that at Salamis in 480 BCE the Persian fleet, led by Phoenician triremes, suffered problems with crosswinds due to their high superstructures, which were probably of a similar design.

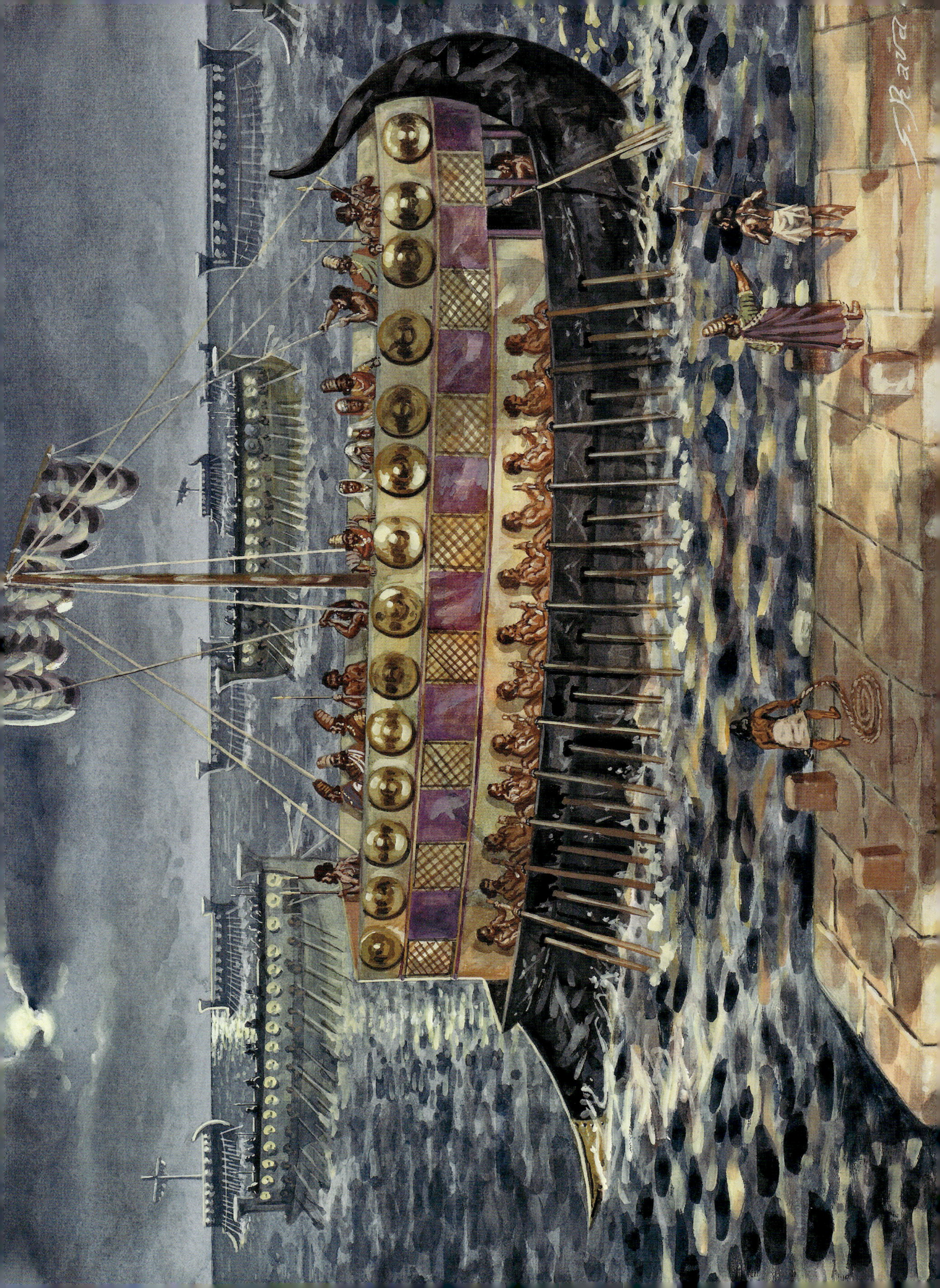

Simplified rigging of an ancient warship. A = Sail; B = Mast; C = Yard; D = Forestay; E = Backstay; F = Lift; G = Sheet; H = Brail; I = Halyard. (Drawing by the author)

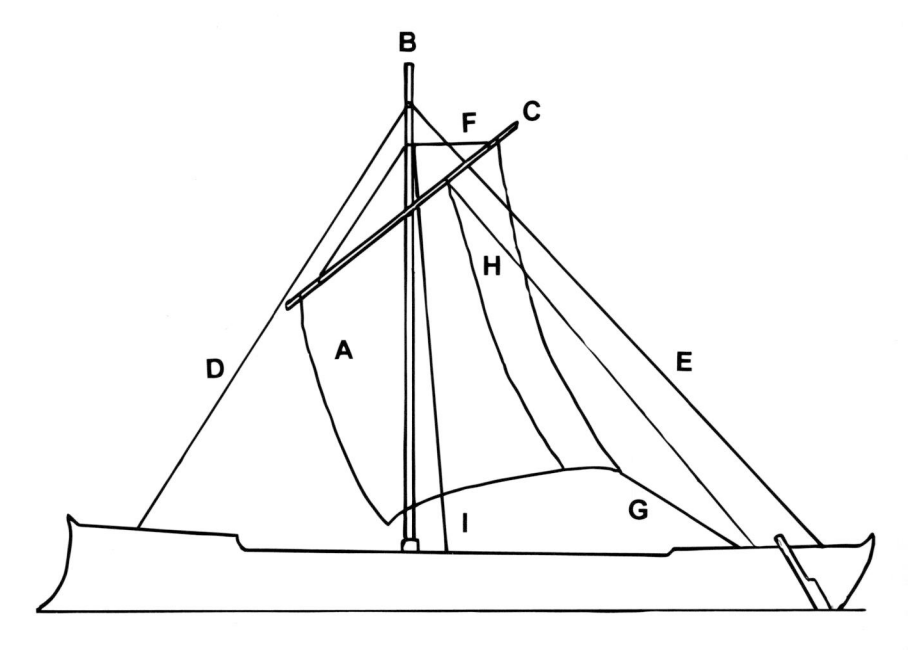

evidence of the use of foreign soldiers by the Carthaginians, Sennacherib armed the Phoenician-built and -manned ships he sent into the Red Sea with his own soldiers, as did Xerxes, the idea being to combine Phoenician seamanship with the fighting power of their own loyal troops.

Josephus [*Jewish Antiquities* IX.14.2] recounts a sea battle fought between several Phoenician cities and Tyre after the latter refused to surrender to Shalmaneser of Assyria. The account reinforces why the monarchs of land powers needed to keep on good terms with the cities of the coast:

> ... when the Tyrians would not submit to him, the king returned, and fell upon them again, while the Phoenicians had furnished him with threescore ships, and eight hundred men to row them; and when the Tyrians had come upon them in twelve ships, and the enemy's ships were dispersed, they took five hundred men prisoners, and the reputation of all the citizens of Tyre was thereby increased.

GREECE

Homeric warlords, warriors and ships

The collapse of Minoan and Mycenaean civilization occurred at the end of the second millennium BCE, about the same time as the migrations of the Sea Peoples. The next few hundred years are a 'dark age' in the Aegean, a time when writing was forgotten and palaces were no longer built. Trade between Greece and the east became monopolized by the Phoenicians and the legacy of Minoan culture was largely forgotten. But the Aegean did not stagnate in this period. Waves of new peoples settled in Greece, causing the natives to immigrate to the coast of Asia Minor. Perhaps more importantly, iron came into regular use as a war material.

The major sources for this period are the epic poems of Homer: the *Iliad* and the *Odyssey*. While they were probably written down in the 8th century BCE, much of their cultural and technological material relates to preceding centuries, passed down as oral poetry. Some aspects, such as a pan-Hellenic war against Troy, may even date from the Mycenaean period, but enough of the technology mentioned by Homer can be dated to the early Iron Age to make references to seafaring a source for the 10th to the 8th centuries. Even the histories of the Classical period do not detail the maritime technology of their time to the same extent.

A 'king' (*basileus*) in Homer was the lord of a small domain, his power measured by the number of warriors he could muster. In return for their support, warriors could influence their king in his choice of policy, as Odysseus relates while in disguise [*Od.* XIV.288]:

> I had nine times had my own command and led a well-found fleet against a foreign land. As a result large quantities of loot fell into my hands ... and my fellow countrymen learned to fear and respect me ... and they pressed me and the famous Idomeneus to lead the fleet to Ilium. There was no way of avoiding it: public opinion was too much for us.

To retain power the king was obliged to provide an opportunity for booty, like a pirate of later times. Warriors contributed to a raid both in battle and by manning the oars of the king's ships.

These then were the types of campaign practised by Greeks of the period: piracy and amphibious raids. Thucydides [I.7] says,

> ... Hellenes and the barbarians of the coast and islands, as communication by sea became more common, were tempted to turn pirates, under the command of their most powerful men... They would fall upon a town unprotected by walls and consisting of a mere collection of villages, and would plunder it; indeed, this came to be the main source of their livelihood, no disgrace being yet attached to such an achievement, but even some glory.

The coast of Ithaca, home of the hero of the *Odyssey*, Odysseus. A rugged land typical of Ionian islands, Ithaca was renowned throughout the ancient world for its connection to Odysseus. During the Mycenaean period Ithaca may have been the centre of a political entity that included islands and parts of the mainland nearby. (Photo courtesy of Hazel Wood)

Eighth century Greek *krater* with a painting of a warship. The ship is a *dikrotos*, with two banks of oars, and may be the first Greek representation of such a vessel. The bow of the ship has a cutwater to decrease wave making and to serve as a ram. The curving stempost and the bulwark around the bow platform are typical of Greek ships of the period. (Author's collection)

In this they were closer to the nomadic warrior bands of their ancestors than to the settled citizens of the Classical world, but as in other periods, it also meant that they controlled their own maritime region. To quote Thucydides [I.13] again,

> Agamemnon ... had also a navy far stronger than his contemporaries... Now Agamemnon's was a continental power; and he could not have been master of any except the adjacent islands ... but through the possession of a fleet.

Though there are no accounts of battles at sea, there is evidence in Homer that these did occur frequently enough to affect the weapons carried aboard ship.

Early pentekonters

The main ship of this period was the *pentekonter*, a vessel rowed by 50 oarsmen. The pentekonter was designed to be used in multiple roles – as a pirate ship, a warship and a trading vessel. This does not mean that all pentekonters of the time were identical. There would be variations in length, beam and appearance, and it is likely that some had a few more or less oars than others. This would depend on when and where a ship was built, and which of its various roles the shipbuilders thought was the most important.

The shape of the pentekonter was basically that of a longboat, similar in some ways to later Viking vessels. It had no deck (described poetically as 'hollow') so that the rowing benches and cargo were exposed to the elements, or as Thucydides says, 'equipped in the ancient fashion, more like pirate craft'. Homer describes it as being both 'capacious' and 'swift'. There were half-decks at either end for the steersman and the lookout. Its bow and stern were symmetrical, reminiscent of a pair of bull's horns. A pentekonter did however have the projecting forefoot synonymous with later Greek warships. As yet this was of oak, not bronze, though it would have been sufficient to damage an enemy ship if driven into its side. The pentekonter was not high like contemporary Phoenician warships; the *Iliad* tells how Hector grasped the top of the stern of a ship while standing on the beach and how Ajax jumped down from the gunwale onto the sand.

E

PENTEKONTER (TOP) AND HEKATONTER (BOTTOM)
The pentekonter was the standard ship used in Greece during the 'Dark Age'. Ships depicted on Geometric pottery show both the distinctive curving 'horns' and the platforms beneath them at bow and stern often enough for them to be diagnostic. The rowers sat on benches in the hull, not at this time covered by a deck, while a rail along the gunwale was common. The 'cutwater', the precursor of the ram, also had a distinctive narrow point which was later to become more robust as ramming became the standard naval tactic. The hekatonter has been reconstructed here as a ship with two banks of 25 oarsmen on each side. The ship was a development of the pentekonter, with the rail of the latter replaced by stanchions to support the upper bank of rowers and the addition of a gunwale on which to rest their oars. Like the pentekonter the ship has a black hull from its coating of pitch, though upper sections of the structure are painted. The emblem on the sail is the club of Heracles, the symbol of Thebes, foremost of Boeotian cities. It is assumed that 20 of the crew were officers or seamen rather than rowers.

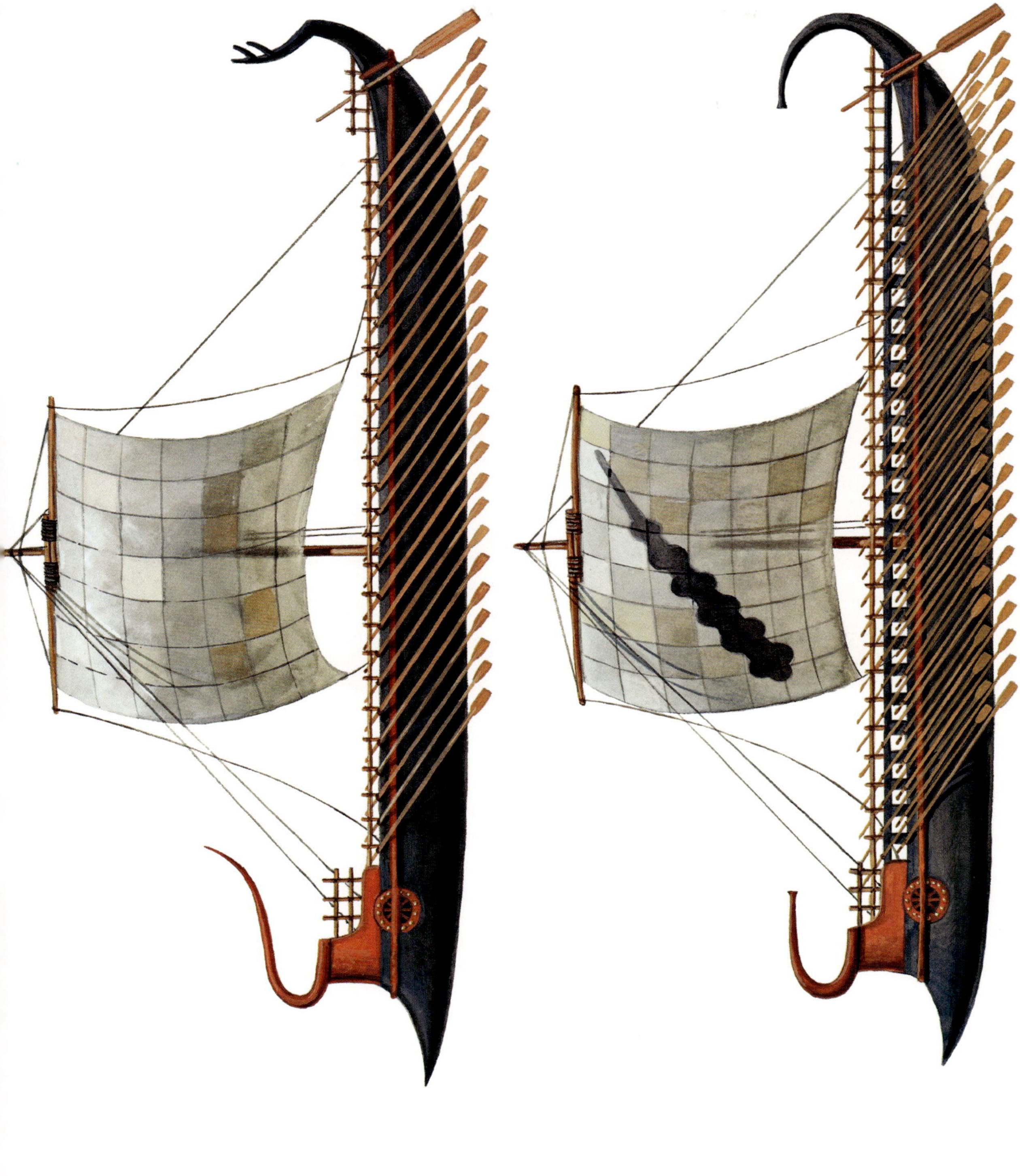

The size of an early pentekonter can be estimated from the number of rowers. Vitruvius relates that the *interscalmium* (the space required for each rower) of a galley was two cubits (approximately 1m). To accommodate 25 men on each quarter, the ship would need to be 26m long at the waterline, to which must be added 3m for the prow and stern. As for beam, wooden ships become more fragile and unstable the greater the (waterline) length-to-beam ratio. To some extent the strength was increased by the use of *hypozomata* ('under-girds'), ropes which helped keep sections of the hull rigid. A narrow ship also allowed very little space for cargo, supplies and so on and Homer describes the ships as 'rounded on both sides', that is, having rounded bilges. The minimum beam for a pentekonter would then be around 2.2m in order to accommodate the rowing benches and a gangway and to comply with Homer's description. Such a ship would have a hull depth of over a metre, half draft and half freeboard. With crew and a supply of food and water aboard it would displace about 12 tonnes.

Homeric ships were black due to the tar with which they were coated. Areas near the prow (sometimes referred to as 'cheeks') were coloured purple, blue or more often red, and many Geometric pots show a curious wheel-like decoration at the same point, perhaps the precursor to the eye design on Classical ships. Sails were white and assembled from pieces of linen sewn together due to the difficulty of weaving a single piece of sailcloth 8m wide. This also made the sail easier to repair in the event of it being damaged.

The construction of ships in Homer varies between the two poems, suggesting that the *Iliad* was composed earlier than the *Odyssey*. In the *Iliad* they are of carvel construction with the planks bound by cords (*sparta*) which after nine years at Troy came loose as the timbers rotted. In the *Odyssey* the construction is mortise and tenon, with the planks connected by dowel-pins (Hesiod's 'many-pegged ships'). Timbers used included poplar, pine and fir. The keel was attached outside the hull after construction and ended in the forefoot (*steira*), which was made of oak to withstand being beached and in case of the need to ram another vessel. At the rear of the hull was a stern-platform (*ikria*) where the steersman sat. The stern itself rose up into the horn-like shape (*aphlaston*) seen in representations of ships on Geometric pottery. The term *ikria* also referred to the bow platform where the lookout would stand and where spears are shown on several contemporary illustrations. Since galleys were beached stern-first and combat on the beach in the *Iliad* is around the stern, this suggests that they were used for actions against other ships rather as much as for amphibious landings.

The steersman handled the tiller (*oieion*) with which he controlled either one or two steering oars (*pedalion*). The rowers sat upon benches (*zuga*) under which supplies and booty were stored in the absence of a covered cargo hold. The fir-wood oars (*eretma*) were run through leather hoops attached to thole-pins (*kleides*). When the rowers needed to reverse oars to move the ship backward (*proeression*) they would have twisted the hoop to the opposite side of the thole-pin to be able to use it as a fulcrum.

The single pine or fir mast (*histos*) of an early pentekonter was probably about 10–11m high with a square-rigged sail (*histion*) suspended from a yard (*epikrion*). The mast could be struck by raising it from its footing (*histopede*) and laying it on a crutch (*histodoke*) with the foot of the mast secured in a crossbeam (*mesodme*). A number of cables (*hoopla*) plaited from leather or papyrus – forestays (*protonoi*), backstays (*epitonis*), brailing ropes (*pous*) and shrouds – served to secure and control the mast and sail. Though a simpler system than the one used on later sailing ships, it allowed the crew to conduct the procedures necessary to sail a simple square-rigged ship in most conditions. Odysseus 'fenced his ship from stem to stern with wicker mats to keep out the waves', a sensible precaution with such a low freeboard. These screens also protected the oarsmen from arrows and other missiles.

Although whenever possible a ship was berthed in harbour (or sometimes moored at sea using *eunai* or anchor stones), the usual method of landing was to beach it stern-first. It was secured by mooring ropes (*peisma*), which could be cut if a rapid departure was required. If the stay was for a longer period, and during winter when ships were usually laid up ashore, a channel was cut for the keel and 'shores' of stones (*hermata*) were piled up to either side of the hull.

Hekatonters

In the catalogue of the fleet in the *Iliad*, the other type of ships mentioned alongside the pentekonters are the 50 ships of the Boeotian contingent: '... in each went a hundred and twenty young men.' The name for these ships used by Pollux is *hekatonter*, meaning a ship of a hundred oars. Homer never uses the word, which was a scholarly term coined later, as was 'pentekonter'. Since there is no other record of a ship with more than 50 oars until the trireme, some modern authors have dismissed Homer's description as exaggeration or fantasy. Yet Thucydides, who lived only a few centuries after the *Iliad* was written down and was also an admiral, had no difficulty accepting Homer's assertion. He believed that the references to ships of 50 and 120 crew were meant to convey the minimum and maximum complements. He understood that ships with more than 50 oars were not beyond the limits of shipbuilding technology prior to the trireme of his own era. It is highly unlikely that shipbuilders went from 50 to 120 oars in a single leap; it is more likely that a number of different configurations and sizes were tried and discarded but that the only reference to them that has survived is in the *Iliad*.

There are a variety of possible explanations to account for the hekatonter, aside from exaggeration or error. Some modern writers have claimed that the ships were pentekonters carrying 70 men in addition to their crew, but this seems unlikely when the size of the pentekonter is considered. One hundred and twenty men in a warship designed for 50 would have had a dangerous effect on its sea-keeping qualities. It is noticeable that the Boeotian contingent has pride of place in Homer's list and it may be that the size of their ships contributed to this.

If most of the complement were rowers or seamen, there are a number of ways in which they could be accommodated by the use of different oar systems. The ships could be *dikrotos*, with two banks of oars one above the other. This became the eventual development of the pentekonter, though the only known representation of such a ship from this period is poorly depicted. Another possibility would be that two men sat next to each other on each side of the ship, each man with a separate oar. This was a system used in the Renaissance, but those galleys were very different in construction and usage and there is no evidence for such a system in the ancient period. Finally, two men could have sat next to each other (on both sides of the ship) and worked the same oar (or 'sweep'). Again this is not known for the period, though later this system was used on very large ships.

Taking the first option it is easy to imagine how the addition of a second bank above the first would be a logical method of increasing the crew size without creating a vessel of unwieldy length. Since 25 rowers in each bank required no more space than in a pentekonter, the waterline length of the ship taken up by oarsmen would not need to be increased above 26m. The beam would be a little wider (around 2.5–3m) and the hull depth would increase to more than 1.5m. It would require *hypozomata* to strengthen the hull, particularly if it was an early attempt to construct a larger ship and stretched the shipbuilding techniques of the day.

Such a vessel would deserve pride of place in a fleet. While it would be heavier than a pentekonter, displacing about 14 tonnes fully laden, the increased oar power would to some extent compensate for this. The larger crew would make it a dangerous vessel to engage and also provide a higher platform for the firing of arrows against smaller vessels, an important factor in later warships.

Eikosoroi

The only ship-type given a specific name in the Homeric poems is the *eikosoros*, making it the earliest use of a technical term for a Greek ship. The word literally means 'equipped with 20 oars'. It is described in the *Odyssey* as, 'a black eikosoros, a broad merchantman which crosses the mighty deep', though it could serve as a military despatch vessel and general runabout. The eikosoros is mentioned in literature of the Classical period, usually as a much larger 'sailing galley' (a compromise between a warship and a sailing ship). The application of the name to larger vessels does not preclude Homer's eikosoroi being small; the term became synonymous with 'wide' due to the description noted above, since the Homeric poems established many aspects of later Greek culture.

A reconstruction of the eikosoros would include these features: it must be propelled by 20 oars, be broad compared to a pentekonter, and consistent with the technology of the time. The rowing area would be at least 10m long, but if oars were considered secondary to the sail there would be less need to squeeze the rowers into the smallest possible space. The waterline length could therefore be 15m (for a total of 17m). At a length-to-beam ratio of 5:1 to account for its noteworthy width, the eikosoros had a beam of 3m, which would make it slow compared to a pentekonter. To be stable enough to travel across open water (hazardous for ancient warships) and to carry sufficient cargo, the freeboard would need to be high for its length, perhaps as much as 1m from a total hull depth of between 1.5–2m. A ship of this size might carry 15 tonnes of cargo in a volume of about 12m x 2m x 1m.

In war the eikosoros would still be of value, despite its low speed. Soldiers, especially archers, were often carried aboard merchant ships in antiquity. It would also serve as an auxiliary vessel, carrying weapons or supplies and in battle picking up men from sunken ships, either for rescue if friendly or as captives if enemy.

F — HOMERIC LANDING

The Greeks of the 'Homeric' period commonly attacked one another's settlements by sea, seeking booty, livestock and slaves. The pentekonter beached stern-first to allow for a rapid departure before local defences could be mobilized. The steersman stands ready with a long pike to help defend the ship if necessary. By his side is a boarding ladder, shown on a number of Greek illustrations. Most of the warriors carry the *dipylon* shield, characteristic of the time.

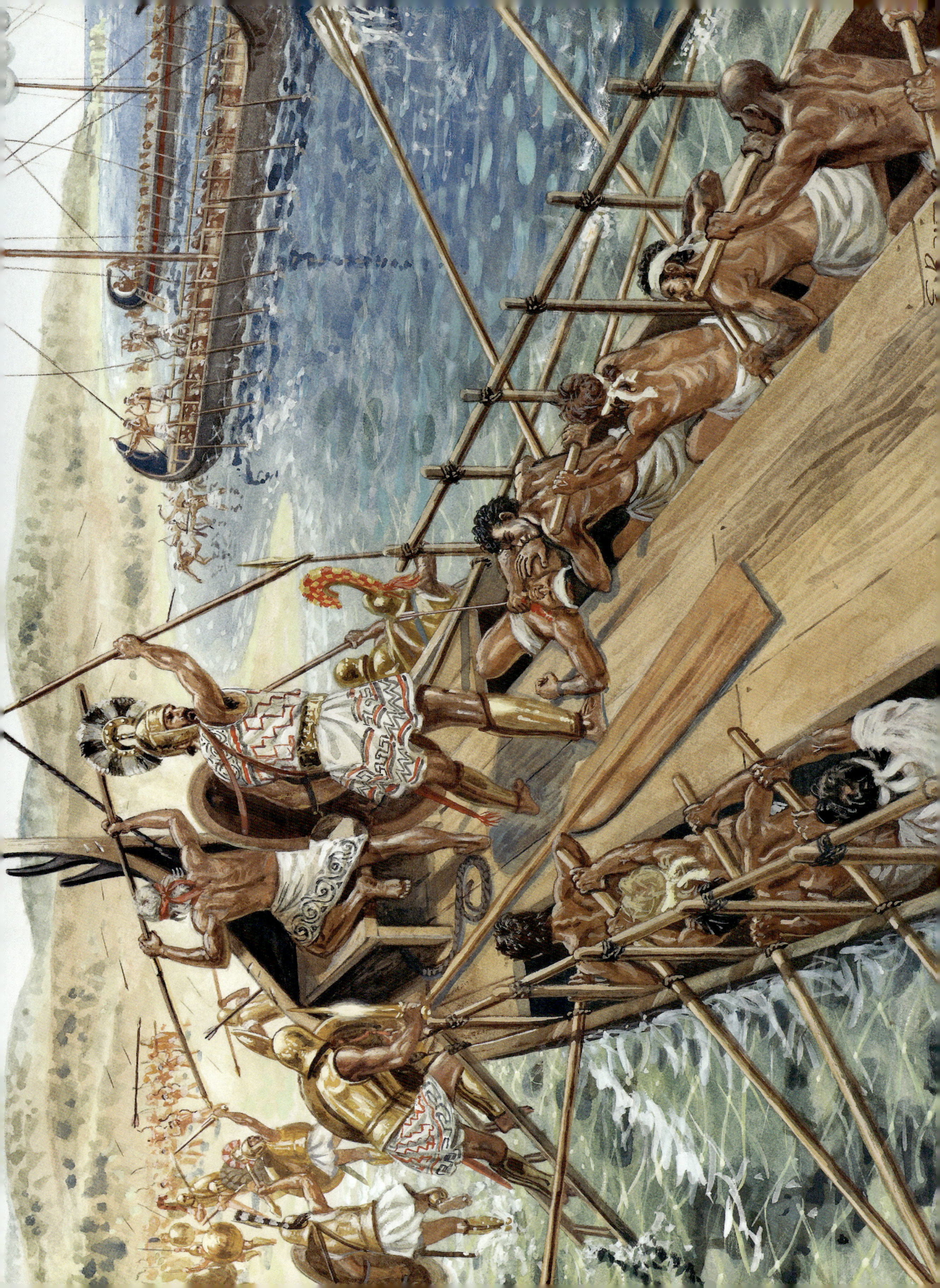

Sixth century pottery model of a ship from Amathus in Cyprus. The combination of oar-ports and the rounded shape of the vessel suggest that this is a 'sailing galley', a type that served as a fleet auxiliary throughout the ancient period and to which Homer's *eikosoros* belonged. (Author's collection)

Homeric tactics

When Thucydides describes naval tactics of his time (the 5th century BCE) he makes it plain that the 'ancient fashion' consisted of boarding, with battles decided by hand-to-hand fighting. For most of ancient history this was the usual method of naval combat, even during the period when ramming was dominant. Thucydides also makes it clear that 'All on board were at once rowers and fighting men.' The simple equipment of the period – shield and spear, and for the wealthier men armour and helmet – were perfectly adequate for this purpose.

Homer also mentions pikes, used by the Greeks when defending their beached ships against attack from land, 'great poles built up of many lengths and tipped with bronze which they kept on board for fights at sea'. The mighty Ajax, strong even among semi-divine heroes, wielded a pike 22 cubits (11m) long. Even accounting for heroic exaggeration, this type of weapon would be useful in the first stages of a boarding action, as was the case even after the introduction of gunpowder. Long spears or pikes are positioned in both the bow and stern of ships depicted on Geometric pottery, though their size is difficult to estimate due to stylistic distortion of scale.

Greek and Phoenician colonies in the Mediterranean. The two cultures in most cases kept to distinct spheres of influence. Friction arose when their interests clashed, as at the battle of Alalia, the result of Greek colonization of Corsica. (Map by David Taylor)

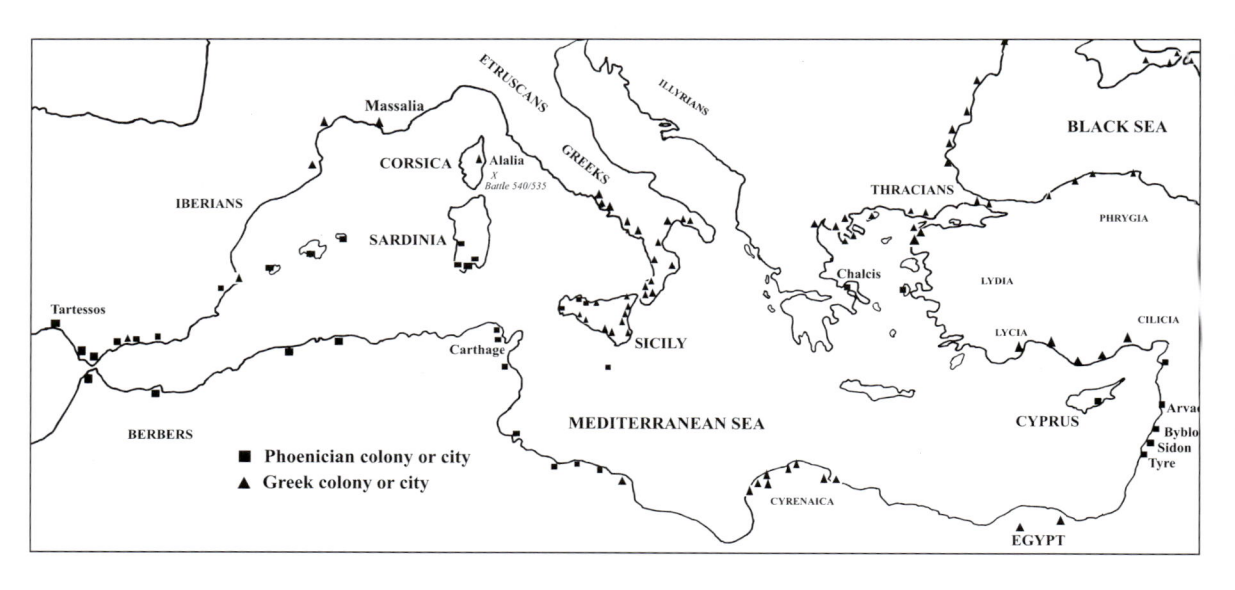

Archery was also employed. Philoctetes' ships were manned by 'fifty oarsmen trained to go into battle with the bow'. Archers are mentioned using poisoned arrows, common in ancient history, which would increase the effectiveness of archery at sea as much as on land.

Some of the Greek contingents were organized into flotillas of 50 ships, further subdivided into squadrons of ten. These squadrons were each commanded by an *archos* (pl. *archoi*), a term which also meant 'captain'.

Colonial wars (*c.* 700–500 BCE)

Although naval engagements were not unknown at the start of the Archaic period – the Chalcidian hero Amphidamus died 'fighting by sea' in the Lelantine war – an important influence on the development of ships in the Aegean was the practise of colonization. As with the Phoenicians the initial reason for colonization was to enable trade, but increases in the population of Greek cities by the end of the 8th century BCE led to the practise of founding new cities abroad. This system was so deeply ingrained that as late as the fifth century cities threatened by the Persians considered moving their entire population by sea to safer locations. Greek mercenaries were also in demand abroad, from Egypt to Tartessos in Spain, and their transport required significant numbers of ships. Inevitably some of these wandering mercenaries turned to piracy, which along with competition for trade led to conflict with Phoenicians and Etruscans. It then became essential that vessels used to transport mercenaries and trade goods could also serve as warships.

Late pentekonters

As in the Homeric period the pentekonter was the standard ship, mainly due to its versatility. Ships relying solely on sail were rare and there was no ancient Greek term that referred to sailing as a method of propulsion; a common term for sailing ships was *holkas*, or 'towed barge', due to the fact that they were often towed behind galleys. The pentekonter on the other hand, in addition to its use as a warship, could still carry some cargo or passengers.

During the 6th century BCE changes occurred to the pentekonter that, while reducing its effectiveness for ancillary tasks, improved it as a pure warship. These were the development of the ram and the addition of a fighting deck and a second bank of oars. These innovations were depicted ever more frequently on pottery and appear to go hand in hand.

The use of the ram as a dedicated weapon may ironically have developed on ships carrying cargo. A ram was intended to sink an enemy vessel and so was of no use to pirates who needed to capture and pillage their prey to make a living. But a ram mounted on a trading ship would have served as a deterrent to a pirate attack. A full deck running between stern and bow platforms appeared on trading ships as a way to protect cargo from the elements. A deck would initially have been mounted on the beams, which previously served as the supports for rowing benches, requiring the shipwright to find a place for the rowers. This could either be below (if the deck and gunwale were raised) or placed upon the deck, leading to the development of two banks of oars, the upper bank being rowed through a *parexeiresia* or outrigger. Ships with decks were known as *cataphract* (as opposed to *aphract*). All of these innovations combined to lead to the development of a new type of warship with increased combat capability.

Corinthian helmet of the late 7th to early 6th century BCE, the favoured helmet of the Archaic period. It maximized protection at the cost of obstructing the wearer's vision and hearing. (Author's collection)

Since the interscalmium dictated the length of a galley, a doubling of the number of oars per unit of length led to a much shorter 50-oared vessel, with considerable advantages. The reduction in the 'wetted area' of the hull meant increases in speed, acceleration and, most importantly for a ship requiring manoeuvrability for effective ramming, rate of turn. In addition it would be much cheaper in terms of timber for the hull and far more robust, dispensing with the need for hypozomata and extending the ship's service, again effectively reducing its cost. By only manning one bank of oars, a ship could still carry a significant amount of cargo or troops. Against these factors must be weighed the smaller area from which warriors or archers could fight, reinforcing the use of ramming instead of boarding tactics.

There were a few changes to the gear carried by a later pentekonter. The steersman's seat was now named *hedolia* and oars were called *kope*, while a bank of oars was known as a *tarsos* (a reference to the city of Tarsus in Cilicia, showing where the Greeks learned some of their nautical lore). Homeric anchor stones were replaced by iron anchors while boarding ladders, especially useful for rapid disembarkation on hostile coasts, were routinely carried. Bow screens are often depicted on contemporary art and side screens (*parablema*) were used in rough seas, fastened to the gunwale below the parexeiresia. Rails were usually employed, improving safety for the crew and providing an obstacle to enemies attempting to board.

A large box-like footing seated the base of the mast (*laiphos*) within the hull. A 6th century wreck excavated off the Mediterranean coast of France has revealed that the mast was slotted over one of the ribs without pegs or nails. This would allow the rapid striking of the mast for battle or in case of a sudden storm. Depictions of the sailing rig from this period reveal an improved method for shortening sail. Brailing ropes, attached along the foot of the sail, ran up and over the yard and down the rear of the sail where they could be easily handled. The ram (*embolos*), originally a cutwater that reduced wave making and thus increased speed, was now sheathed in bronze. Apart from the obvious advantage in ramming, this would also help protect it from wear on beaching and allow removal of the bronze for repairs without having to replace the wood itself.

A reconstruction of a dikrotos pentekonter shows significant improvements in performance over the earlier *monokrotos* type. The waterline length would be reduced from 26m to 18m (reducing the total from 29m to 21m), with only a marginal increase in beam to 2.3m. The draft would remain at 0.6m while the freeboard would increase from 0.6m to 1m, providing an extra edge in boarding actions and height for firing missiles.

G — BATTLE OF ALALIA

The plate shows a reconstruction of the battle with a dikrotos pentekonter of the Phokaians ramming the side of an Etruscan monokrotos pentekonter. Both ships have the same number of oarsmen, but the Phokaian vessel has its rowers concentrated into a much shorter hull, increasing manoeuvrability, the essential factor in ramming. The Etruscans, however, though outmanoeuvred, have the advantage of a longer deck, allowing more men to take part in either the casting of missiles or a boarding melee. Ramming techniques were later refined (probably by attacking at a more acute angle) to reduce damage to the ramming ship.

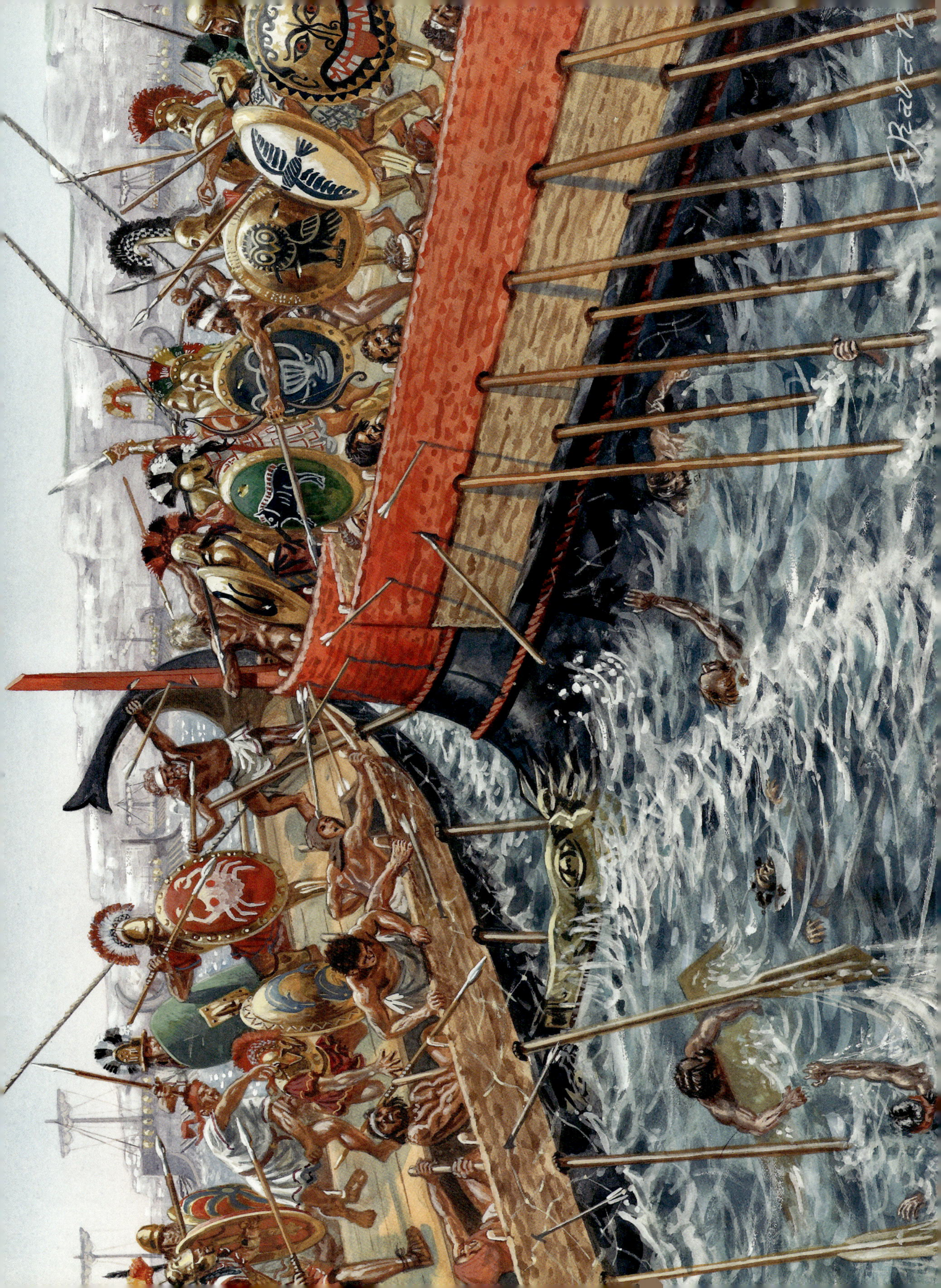

These factors combine to produce a vessel both lighter (9.5 tonnes compared to 12 tonnes) and faster (increasing maximum speed by around a knot to 5.5 knots). It would also accelerate over 25 per cent faster and turn twice as quickly, for only 80 per cent of the cost of the earlier type.

Triakonters

Many early Mediterranean galleys were rowed by 30, probably the optimum size in terms of construction cost and time, berthing requirements, crewing and performance. Throughout the Archaic and Classical periods contemporary sources mention 30-oared ships and even when the pentekonter became the standard auxiliary naval vessel, *triakonters* were still used. Illustrations depict them with the same lines and configuration as other Greek ships, and bearing a similar ram, but with only 15 oars a side.

A triakonter would have a waterline length of about 17.5m and a breadth of 2.2m, only marginally smaller than a dikrotos pentekonter. However with a shallower hull and smaller crew, the triakonter would weigh only 7 tonnes. In terms of performance it would be slower than a monokrotos pentekonter but have improved acceleration and rate of turning. A triakonter would be used as a despatch vessel, for reconnaissance, and also for rescuing sailors from sunk or damaged ships. While its value offensively was minor, it compensated with enhanced manoeuvrability, allowing it to easily turn to avoid being rammed. It is this that allowed them to remain in service when warships were growing ever larger. Not worth the effort of pursuit, triakonters could wait out of bowshot until needed, perhaps also daring to ram and finish off ships already crippled if the opportunity arose.

Archaic tactics and the battle of Alalia

One of the most noteworthy of the Greek cities involved in the early colonization of the Western Mediterranean was Phokaia in Ionia, which at its height boasted a fleet of 120 pentekonters. Since dikrotos vessels were believed to have been invented at Erythrae, only 32km from Phokaia, it is certain that Phokaian ships would be of this advanced type. After colonizing Massalia

A black-figure *dinos krater* from Attica, made during the 6th century BCE. The ships are pentekonters, though each has a different number of oars showing that the number of rowers varied. It is likely that the number of oars depended upon the number of oarsmen available. (Bridgeman)

around 600 BCE, Phokaia founded Alalia, on Corsica, from where they encroached upon Etruscan and Carthaginian interests, initially through trade and the provision of mercenaries but later through piracy. This led to an engagement known as the battle of Alalia in about 540 to 535 BCE, described by Herodotus [I.166–7]:

> Then, since they plundered the property of all their neighbours, the Tyrrhenians and Carthaginians made expedition against them by agreement with one another, each with sixty ships. And the Phokaians also manned their vessels, sixty in number, and came to meet the enemy in that which is called the Sardinian sea: and when they encountered one another in the sea-fight the Phokaians won a kind of Cadmean victory, for forty of their ships were destroyed and the remaining twenty were disabled, having had their prows bent aside.

This is the first instance in which the use of ramming tactics was recorded. It is certain that the Etruscan and Carthaginian ships were also equipped with rams, since the destruction of 40 Phokaian ships could only have been accomplished by ramming tactics; vessels taken by boarding would certainly have been captured as prizes. Yet only damage to the Phokaian rams is mentioned. This may be because their ships, and their rams, were better constructed, but it is also possible that the reason for the damage to the victorious ships was that they used the *diekplous*, the preferred naval tactic for the next few centuries.

Half a century later, when the Ionians mustered to resist Persia, it was a Phokaian, Dionysius, who was given command of the combined fleet, despite his city contributing only three out of 353 ships. This was probably due to the experience that the Phokaians had in naval warfare and, along with the punishing training that Dionysius imposed on the other Ionians, he may have taught them the diekplous. If this is the case then it may have been the use of this tactic at Alalia that damaged the rams of the Phokaian ships. The diekplous consisted of ships in a line abreast passing through the gaps in the enemy line then making a rapid turn to attack on the enemies' vulnerable quarter or stern. A ram striking an enemy ship moving laterally (at perhaps five or six

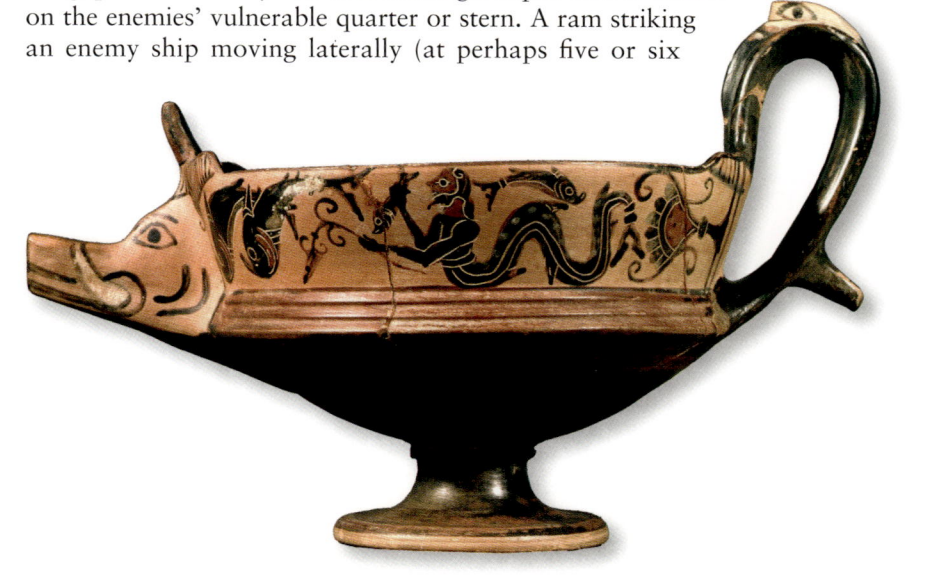

This *kyathos*, dating from between 575 and 550 BCE, the height of the Greek colonizing period, is shaped and painted to resemble a boar-snouted boat. The fact that a vase or ladle was shaped to resemble a ship of this design suggests that the boar-shape must have been a familiar sight before the first *Samaina* was built. (Bridgeman)

knots) could easily be damaged or torn away by the conflicting forces, particularly since rams were only loosely attached to the hull.

A victory over a fleet twice as large was clearly a triumph for the Phokaians, but the end result was a strategic victory for their enemies. Alalia was immediately abandoned and of the survivors of the 40 destroyed Phokaian vessels, more were taken as captives (and stoned to death) than escaped. In the longer term the Carthaginians and Etruscans secured control of the Western Mediterranean.

Tyrants and sea power

According to Sophocles, the word 'tyrant' derived from the Tyrrhenians (Etruscans), who the Greeks considered cruel and dangerous and 'sank any ship entering their waters'. Greek tyrannies were dictatorships in which one man or family acquired and held power by force. The growth of tyrannies during the 7th and 6th centuries BCE galvanized the growth of Greek sea power by the accumulation of wealth and power into the hands of a single interest, that of reinforcing the tyrant's security and prestige. With the resources of the polis under their control, tyrants not only built and developed stronger naval forces, but also allied with other tyrants for mutual support.

The fleets of poleis such as Phokaia were constituted from privately owned ships used for trade, transport and piratical raids; in Athens nobles called *naukraria* were obliged to provide one ship each for the use of the state. But under the influence of tyrants state-owned ships became more common until they formed the national navies that were the norm in the Classical period. In Corinth tyrants built a state-controlled navy with which they suppressed piracy, allowing an increase in trade and therefore wealth to further support the tyranny. In addition they sold or built ships for other poleis, furthering their strategic aims abroad.

Polycrates and the Samaina

The most renowned tyrant of this period was Polycrates, who ruled Samos from 538 to 522 BCE. Polycrates assembled a force of 100 pentekonters and 1,000 archers to consolidate his position, protect the lucrative eastern trade in iron and copper, ravage the lands of his enemies and become a major power that flirted with both Egypt and the nascent Persian Empire. He may also have sought to monopolize the export of mercenaries to Egypt, in which Samos had long been involved. One hundred pentekonters cost one talent a day to operate, or seven to eight tonnes of silver per year, causing Polycrates to seek the support of Egypt to help to pay for his navy.

H — TRIAKONTER (TOP) AND SAMAINA (BOTTOM)

The triakonter was the smallest warship used by the ancient Greeks. It had probably been in service in one form or another since the Mycenaean period, and survived as a scout and dispatch vessel long after the appearance of the trireme. It was in effect a smaller version of the pentekonter, fitted with only 30 oars and constructed and equipped as lightly as possible to enhance its speed. The Samaina of the tyrant Polycrates was intended to combine the capabilities of the dikrotos pentekonter with an increased cargo-carrying capacity. The substantial 'boar-like' bow, in which the ram formed the boar's snout, must have been intended for ramming, while the full deck enhanced the crew's ability to fight without becoming entangled with oarsmen and rowing benches and also protected the cargo from the elements. Within 50 years the Samaina was surpassed in both roles, by triremes, and by larger sailing ships.

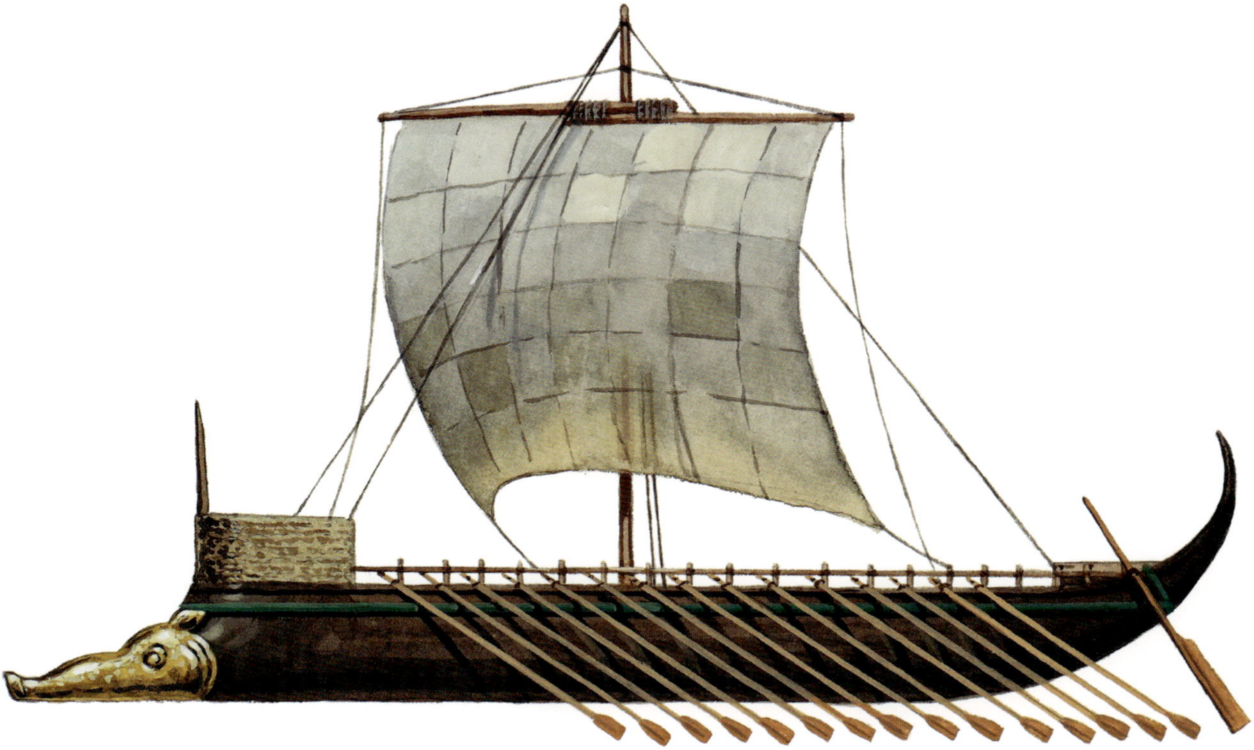

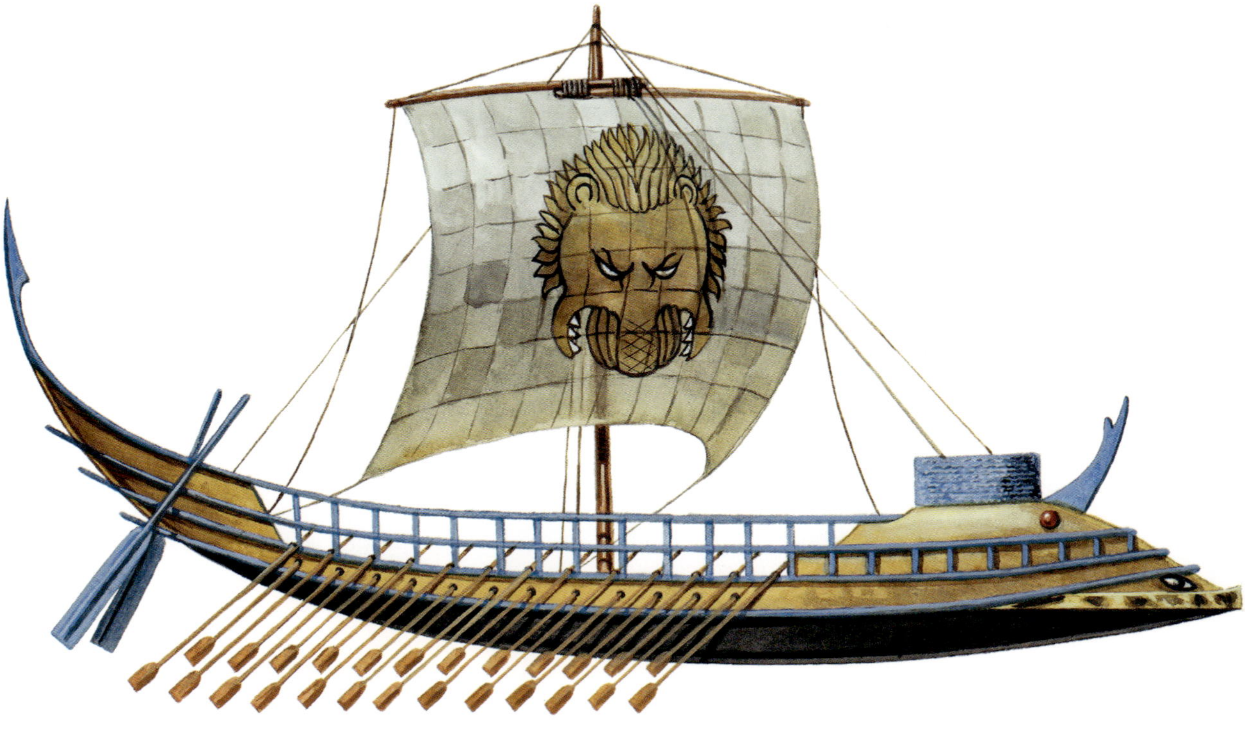

TOP
Painting on a late 6th century Greek pot of a vessel fitting the description of Polycrates' *Samaina*; it has the boar-like snout, including a robust ram, and two banks of oars. Note the very high bulwark on the bow platform. The lower oars are rowed through ports, the upper bank rest on the gunwale but below the double rail. (Alamy)

BELOW
Painted around the time of Polycrates' tyranny by Nikosthenes, this Attic black-figure cup shows two boar-snouted ships under sail. The complex structure of the rams is clearly visible as are the bow officers (*proreus*) and the ladders at the stern for disembarkation. (Bridgeman)

In addition Polycrates, according to Athenaeus, 'summoned craftsmen at very high rates of pay... Polycrates was the first man to build ships and name them Samian after his country.' These ships, *Samaina*, have been described in detail and an estimation of their appearance, capabilities and purpose is possible. The Samaina was a *ploion dikroton*, that is a ship with two banks of oars. According to Plutarch it combined the qualities of a galley with a sailing ship: it could 'race' under oars and was slender at the bow, but could also negotiate high seas under sail due to its broad beam. Didymos relates that the ship was fully decked while other sources mention its similarity to a boar. Contemporary illustrations, including those on coins from the Samian colony of Zankle, show the forward section of ships in which the prow and ram (with a particularly blunt, snout-like terminus) are shaped to resemble a boar.

These sources are describing what was later known as a *histiokopos*, a 'sailing galley' with a capacious cargo hold which could double as a warship at need. For the purposes of Polycrates – the transport of goods and soldiers and the ability to fight with ram or marines (*epibatai*) – the Samaina would be an ideal compromise.

A reconstruction based on a 6:1 hull-to-beam ratio results in a ship 26m long and 4.6m wide. Two banks of oars and a deck result in a freeboard of 2.5m, which would give an advantage in boarding actions over lower vessels. Nevertheless it would be a stable vessel able to carry 15 tonnes of cargo. While it would be at a disadvantage against a standard dikrotos pentekonter (poorer in speed, acceleration and rate of turning), its ability to operate in a variety of conditions and roles suggest that the Samaina would fulfil Polycrates' intention to use it for gaining 'mastery of the seas'.

The end of an era

By the end of the 6th century BCE naval matters were rapidly evolving in the Aegean and Mediterranean. Many states were changing to new forms of government so that despite the decline of tyrants, the organization of national fleets intended solely for war increased. Rowers, now as valuable to the state as citizen soldiers, began to influence the policies of those states. The rise of the Persian Empire and its control of Phoenician navies increased this as other states sought ways to compete with the new threat. Before the end of his rule, Polycrates' navy adopted triremes, the next development in naval warfare and one that for a thousand years would ensure that pure warships became the norm. The previous two millennia of ships, which were both cargo vessel and warship, gave way to specialization. Not that sailing galleys, pentekonters, triakonters and other early types disappeared; they were too well engrained in ship design, construction and usage for that and survived as auxiliaries and support vessels. But they handed over their trading role to a vast array of sailing craft and their position in the front line of the fleet to ever-larger warships.

BIBLIOGRAPHY

Primary Sources
Herodotus Histories
Hesiod Works and Days
Homer Iliad & Odyssey
Josephus Jewish Antiquities
Plutarch Lives
Strabo The Geography
Thucydides Peloponnesian War
Book of Ezekiel

Select Secondary Sources
Bass, George F., Pulak, Cemal, Collon, Dominique & Weinstein, James, 'The Bronze Age Shipwreck at Ulu Burun: 1986 Campaign' in *American Journal of Archaeology*, Vol. 93 (1989), pp.1–29
Bryce, T., 'The Hittite Deal with the Hiyawa-Men' in Cohen, Y., Gilan, A. & Miller, J. (eds), *Pax Hethitica: Studies on the Hittites and Their Neighbours in Honour of Itamar Singer*, Studien zu den Bogazkoy-Texten Band 51, Wiesbaden, Harrassowitz, pp.47–53
Bryce, T., *The Kingdom of the Hittites*, OUP, Oxford (2005)
Casson, L., *Ships and Seamanship in the Ancient World*, Johns Hopkins University Press, Princeton (1995)
Castleden, R., *Minoans*, Routledge, Abingdon (1993)
Coates, J. F., 'Pentekonters and Triereis Compared' in *Tropis II*, pp.111–116
Davis, N. De G. & Faulkner, R. O., 'A Syrian Trading Venture to Egypt' in *Journal of Egyptian Archaeology*, Vol. 33 (1947), pp.40–46
Finley, M. I., *The World of Odysseus*, Penguin, Harmondsworth (1979)
Gardiner, R. (ed.), *The Earliest Ships*, Conway, London (1996)
Hagy, James W., '800 Years of Etruscan Ships' in *International Journal of Nautical Archaeology and Underwater Exploration*, Vol. 15:3 (1986), pp.221–250
McGrail, S., *Ancient Boats and Ships*, Shire, Princes Risborough (2006)
Miles, R., *Carthage Must Be Destroyed*, Allen Lane, London (2010)
Morrison, J. S., *The Ship: Long Ships and Round Ships*, HMSO, London (1980)
Morrison, J. S., Coates, J. F. & Rankov, N. B., *The Athenian Trireme*, CUP, Cambridge (2000)
Morrison, J. S. & Williams, R. T., *Greek Oared Ships 900–322 B.C.*, CUP, Cambridge (1968)
Tilley, A., *Seafaring on the Ancient Mediterranean* (BAR 1268), Oxford (2004)
Torr, C., *Ancient Ships*, CUP, Cambridge (1895)
Vinson, S., *Egyptian Boats and Ships*, Shire, Princes Risborough (1994)
Wallinga, H. T., *Ships and Sea-power Before the Great Persian War*, Brill, Leiden (1993)

The simple attachment of the mast on ancient ships relied on the interlocking design of the mast socket (A) and the frame in the keel (B), supported by stays fore and aft. Based on the Bon-Porte wreck. (Drawing by the author after Hagy)

INDEX

Numbers in **bold** refer to plates and illustrations

Aegean, the 7, 12, 14, 15, **16**, 19, 22, 25, 26, 30, 39, 46
Agamemnon 32
Ahhiyawa 22
Ajax 32, 38
Alalia, the battle of 5, **38**, **G40**, 42, 43, 44; founding, the 5, 43
Alasiya, the battle of 5, **18**, 23, 24, **24**
Amathus **38**
Amidships, canopied areas 18; raised deck 10; single mast 18
Amphibious landings 6, 19, 34
Amphidamus 39
Anatolia **15**, 16, 20, 22, **23**, **25**
Anchor stones (*eunai*) 23, 35, 40
Antelope's Nose, the battle of 5, 6
Archaic period 39, **40**
Archery 11, **B12**, 14, 15, 19, 27, 39
Arrowhead 17, 19
Arwad **25**
Asia Minor 30
Assyrian frieze **26**
Athenaeus 46
Auxiliary vessels 36, **38**, 42

Backstay (*epitonis*) 2, 10, 27, **27**, **30**, 34
Barges 6, 14, 39
Boarding 11, **17**, 19, 23, 24
Boarding platforms (*holkaion*) 11, 17, 23
Boat design, boar-snouted **43**, **46**; diamond-shaped crosshatching 17; horn-like shape (*aphlaston*) 34; hull depth 34, 36; rounded and reinforced hull **20**; sickle shaped boat 7; 'spoon'-shaped hull 7
Boeotian **E32**, 35
Boom 2, 8, **11**, **17**, 18, 23
Bow 2, 8, **A8**, **11**, **14**, 14, 17, 18, **28**, 32, **32**, **E32**, 34, **38**, **H44**, 46
Bow platform 11, **32**, 34, 39, **46**
Bows 10, **B12**, 39, 42
Bowsprit 2, 18
Braces 18, 27
'Bricklaying' 10
Broad beam **C20**, 46
Bronze Age, the 5, 6, 20, **20**, **C20**, 23, 24
Bulwarks 8, **26**, **32**
Bunting 17
Byblos 6, 24

Cables (*hoopla*) 7, 10, 27, 34
Carians, the 15, 17
Carthage **26**
'Castles' 8, 14
Cilicia 25, 40
Colonial wars 39
Colonization 4, **38**, 39, 42
Copper 15, 20, 44
Corinth 5, 44
Corsica 5, **38**, 43
Cotton 10
Classical period, the 11, 19, 31, 36, 42, 44
Cretans **16**, 17
Crete 7, **15**, 16, **16**, 17, 17, 18, 19, **C20**; Minoan Crete 5, 15, 17
Crossbeams (*mesodme*) 8, 23, 34
Crow's nest 8, 10, 14
Crutch (*histodoke*) 18, 34
Cubits 34, 38
Cutwater 2, **26**, **28**, **D28**, 32, **E32**, 40
Cyclades, the 15, **16**
Cyprus 6, 12, **15**, **18**, 20, **25**, 26

'Dark Age', the 30, **E32**
Delta 6, **A8**; the battle of the 5, 6, 8, 11, **B12**
Diekplous 2, 43
Dikrotos 2, **25**, **32**, 35, 40, **G40**, 42, **H44**, 46
Dionysius 43
Dismantling of ships 8, 11, 26

Eikosoroi 36
Erythrae 42
Etruscans 39, **G40**, 44
Ezekiel, the Book of 25, 26

Fighting deck 2, **25**, **25**, 27, **D28**, 39
Footing (*histopede*) 34, 40
Forefoot 2, 17, 32, 34
Forestay (*protonoi*) 2, 10, 27, **27**, **30**, 34
Freeboard 2, 11, 34, 35, 36, 40, 46
Frescos 5, 6, 7, **16**, 17, 19

Galleys 2, 11, **14**, 26, 34, 35, 39, 40; Classical 11; Egyptian **A8**, 15; Mediterranean 42, 46; Minoan **C20**; sailing (*histiokopos*) 36, **38**, 46
Gangway 8, 10, **17**, 34
Gebel el-Arak knife 5, 8
Gelidonya ship wreck 5, **C20**, 22, **23**
Geometric pottery **E32**, 34, 38
Greece 5, 6, 25, 30, **E32**
Gunwale 2, 8, 10, 14, **17**, 23, 26, 32, **E32**, 39, 40, 46

Halfa grass 10
Halyards 10
Hatshepsut, Queen 5, 11
Hatti 22, 23
Hekatonter **E32**, 35
Helmets, Boar's-tusk helmets 19; Corinthian 40; Homeric **38**; Sea Peoples' 14
Herodotus 8, **10**, 17, 43
Hesiod 34
Hierakonpolis 6, 7
Hittites, the 5, **19**, 22, 24, **24**
Hogging 2, 7
Homer 25, 30, 31, 32, 34, 35, 36, **F36**, **38**, **38**, 39, 40; Achaeans 14; *Iliad* 30, 32, 34, 35; Odysseus 31, **31**, 35; *Odyssey* 30, **31**, 34, 36
Interscalmium 2, 34, 40
Iron 26, 30, 40, 44
Iron Age, the 31
Ischomachus 28
Ithaca 31
Ivory 7, 8, **15**

Knossos 5, **16**
*Krater*s 19, 32, 42

Lelantine War 5, 39
Length-to-beam ratio 23, 36
Levant, the 5, 6, 7, 8, **A8**, **15**, **15**, 16, 20
Lifts 18, 27
Linen 10, 18, 27, 34
Long-range missile weapons 2, 8, **B12**, 14, 23, 35, 40, **G40**
Lookout 32, 34
Lycia (*Lukka*) 22, 25

Marines 8, 10, 11, **D28**, 46
Massalia 5, 42
Masts 8, 11
Masthead 17, 23
Mediterranean 4, 5, 6, 7, **A8**, 10, 20, 22, 25, **38**, 40, 42, 46; Eastern 5, 6, 16, 20, **20**, 24, 25, 28; Western 42, 44
Medinet Habu 7, 8, **A8**, 10, **11**, 12, **B12**, **14**, 15
Mercenaries 10, 17, 20, 22, 28, 39, 43, 44
Merchantman **C20**, 26, 36
Mesopotamia 20, **25**
Minoan Thalassocracy, the 15, 16
Minoans 5, **17**, 18, 19
Minos 15, 16, 17
Monokrotos 2, 40, **G40**, 42
Mortise and tenon joints 8, 22, 26
Mycenaeans, the 16, **19**, 20, 22, 30, 31, **31**, **H44**

New Kingdom, the 6, 7, 8
Nile, the **4**, 5, 6, 7, 11, **11**

Oars 2, 8, 10, 11, **11**, 14, **17**, 18, 26; banks of 2, **25**, 26, **26**, **32**, **E32**, 35, 39, 46, **46**; Phoenician 27; reverse oars 34; steering oars 8, 17, 23, 34; under oars B12, 14, **26**, 27, 46
Oarsmen 11, 18, 32, **E32**, 35, 36, 39, **G40**, 42, **H44**
Old Kingdom, the 6
Outrigger (*parexeiresia*) 2, **26**, 39

Paddles 8, **11**, 18, **C20**
Papyrus **4**, 8, 10, 18, 34
Pentekonters 32, 35, **F36**, 39, 42, **42**, 44, 46

Persians, the 5, 28, **D28**, 39, 43, 44, 46
Phoenicians 5, 6, **18**, 24, 25, **25**, 26, **26**, 27, **27**, 28, **28**, **D28**, 30, 32, **38**, 39, 46
Phokaians 5, **G40**, 42, 43, 44
Pikes 19, 38
Piracy 4, 6, 14, 15, **C20**, 28, 31, 32, 39, 43, 44
Poleis 2, 25, 44
Polycrates 5, 44, 46, **46**
Prows 7, 17, 19, 43
Punt 5, 6

Raid 7, 19, 31
Rails 23, 40
Rameses III, relief of 7, 8, **A8**, 11, **11**, **14**, 14, **15**; warships of 7, 10, 11
Ramming 11, 19, 28, **E32**, 38, 40, **G40**, 43, **H44**
Red Sea, the 7, 8, 30
Rigging 7, 8, **A8**, **11**, **20**, 30
Rope 2, 18, 23, 27; brails/brailing ropes 2, 10, **30**, 34, 40; girdles 7; ladders 23; loops 8; mooring ropes 35; sheet 2, 10, 27, **30**; shroud 2, 35; trusses 22; under-girds 34
Rowers 8, 10, 11, **C20**, 27, **E32**, 34, 35, 36, 38, 39, **G40**, **42**, 46
Rowing benches (*zuga*) 8, **17**, 32, **E32**, 34, 39, **H44**

Sails, Arab-style triangular sail **4**; furled 8, **14**; loose-footed sail 2, **A8**; single sail 23; square-rigged sail (*histion*) 34, 35
Sailcloth **4**, 34
Samaina, the 43, 44, **H44**, 46, **46**
Samos 5, 44
Sea Peoples, the 5, 6, **A8**, 10, **11**, 12, **B12**, **14**, **15**, **C20**, 22, 24, 30, **G40**
Sennacherib 26, 28, 30
Shalmaneser III 5, 30
Shields 19, **26**, 38; *dipylon* **F36**; round 14
Shipbuilding 7, 8, **16**, 20, 25, 35, 36
Sicily **15**, 25
Side screens (*parablema*) **4**, 8, **A8**, 40
Sidonians, The 24, 25, 28
Solomon 5, 25
Spars 2, 10, 23
Spears 10, 14, 19, 34, 38
Stanchions 18, 27, **E32**
Steersman 8, **10**, 18, **C20**, 32, 34, 40
Stempost **24**, **32**
Stern 2, 7, 8, **A8**, 10, **11**, **14**, 17, 18, **28**, 32, **E32**, **34**, 35, **F36**, **38**, 39, 43, **46**
Sternpost 8, 22
Sumerians 7, 8
Suppiluliuma II 5, **18**, 23, 24, **24**
Swords 14, 19
Syrians 5, 12, 14, **15**, 20, **20**, **C20**, 22

Thebes 11, **E32**
Thera **16**, 17, 18, 19
Thucydides 15, 31, 32, 35, 38
Timber 34; cedar 6, 8, 27; conifer 8, 18; cypress 6, 18; ebony 8; fir 23, 26, 34; juniper 8; lime 18; oak 23, 27, 32, 34; pine 8, 34; poplar 34; supplies 5, 6, 7, 8, 10, 16, **18**, 20, **22**, 40
Tin 20, 25
Trading 4, 16, 17, **C20**, 25, 32, 39, 47
Triakonters 42, 47
Triremes 27, **D28**, **H44**, 46
Troy 31, 34
Tudhaliya IV 5, 24
Tuthmosis III 5, 6
Tyrants 44, **H44**, 46
Tyre 5, 24, 25, **25**, 26, **D28**, 30
Tyrians 5, 26, **27**, 28, **D28**, 30
Tyrrhenians 43, 44

Ugarit 5, **19**, **C20**, 22, 23, 24
Uluburun ship wreck 5, **C20**, 22, **22**, 23, **23**, 24

Vikings, the 14, 32

Waterline 2, 17, 34, 36, 40, 42

Xerxes 28, 30

Yardarm 14, 18
Yard (*epikrion*) 2, 10, 23, 27, **30**, 34, 40

48